Parenting made *Easy*

Parenting made Easy

How to Raise Happy Children

sue atkins

Vermilion
LONDON

1 3 5 7 9 10 8 6 4 2

Published in 2012 by Vermilion, an imprint of Ebury Publishing
Ebury Publishing is a Random House Group company

The Random House Group Limited Reg. No. 954009
Addresses for companies within the Random House Group can be found at
www.randomhouse.co.uk

A CIP catalogue record for this book is available from the British Library

The Random House Group Limited supports The Forest Stewardship
Council (FSC®), the leading international forest certification organisation.
Our books carrying the FSC label are printed on FSC® certified paper.
FSC is the only forest certification scheme endorsed by the leading
environmental organisations, including Greenpeace.
Our paper procurement policy can be found at
www.randomhouse.co.uk/environment

Printed and bound by CPI Group (UK) Ltd, Croydon, CR0 4YY

ISBN 9780091940041

Copies are available at special rates for bulk orders. Contact the sales
development team on 020 7840 8487 for more information.

To buy books by your favourite authors and register for offers, visit
www.randomhouse.co.uk

I'd like to dedicate this book to my Mum and Dad, who gave me the gift of self-esteem and so many happy memories of childhood. Thank you, I miss you both.

Contents

Acknowledgements

I'd like to thank all my wonderful friends, especially Nicky Day, Chris Roberts and Sarah Jackson, who have put up with me as I have battled my demons of despair about getting my work 'out there' to a global audience. Thanks for listening while I banged on about my passion for empowering parents with my unique and different techniques and strategies, free from judgement, finger-pointing or criticism. You know it has regularly kept me up very late at night and bouncing out of bed very early in the morning, and I know you may have secretly thought I was mad! Thank you for believing in me.

Also I'd like to thank my extremely long-suffering husband, Kevin, for cooking, cleaning and ironing, plus doing lots of taxiing and pick-ups of our two wonderful teenage kids, while I wrote, blogged, tweeted and did BBC Radio interviews early in the morning and late at night! You have a canny knack for sniffing out commas and spotting my repetition a mile off. Thanks for listening to me – I know I go on a bit!

Special thanks must go to the incredible Kelly Cairns, my wonderful VA, for all her technical help and expertise. I really don't think I ever need to get to grips with that side to my life any more. You are amazing and have never once complained about my late-night emails! Thank you.

And, finally, I'd like to thank all the wonderful parents and children I've had the pleasure of working with throughout my career. Thank you for all your emails, stories and testimonials, and for trusting me with your niggles, worries and problems. I'd like to really thank you for all the beautiful cards, notes and little pressies you have given to me – I have kept them all. You really are the special ones and who this book is for.

sue@TheSueAtkins.com
www.TheSueAtkins.com

Introduction

'A hundred years from now it will not matter what my bank account was, the sort of house I lived in, or the kind of car I drove...but the world may be different because I was important in the life of a child.' – Forest Witcraft

We are the first generation of parents who have had to control, guide, nurture and put boundaries round a technologically savvy, and totally 'connected' generation of children. There is very little preparation for parenting through these very exciting but very new times of 24/7 social media.

We all do our very best as parents, but sometimes we can't see the wood for the trees because we get stuck in the 'socks and pants' of life: focusing on all the trivial details rather than looking up and seeing the bigger picture. Children are all so wonderfully individual and sometimes we need a bit of help, a new idea or a different strategy to navigate the choppy waters of bringing them up – because kids don't come with a handbook!

My intention in writing this book is to help you on your parenting adventure so that you can learn to be and develop into the very best parent you can be, and break free from anxiety, guilt and regret. I'm passionate about parenting and I love helping parents get back into the driving seat of their family relationships, boosting their confidence and putting back the bounce and laughter into their family life again, and this book is a way for me to do just that with you now. I work with parents from all walks of life to create a healthy and happy ethos within their home atmosphere and to ensure that they have a positive environment in which their children can thrive.

My perspective as a Parent Coach is different to the many theories, experts, books, podcasts, DVDs and TV programmes already out there, as I believe that every family is unique, so I aim to support you in discovering that all the answers lie within **you**, and that **you** are the real experts in raising your children.

My expertise and professional training is in helping **you** to bring out **your** answers and gain clarity, direction and confidence in your parenting, in a non-judgemental and non-critical way so that you feel empowered with your own answers and ways of doing things that work for your family. My vision is for you to create a really fulfilling, rewarding and happy family so that your children grow up with fond memories of their childhood. I also want to help you give your children the ultimate gift of self-esteem, true self-belief and inner confidence so that they can flourish and blossom into responsible, well-balanced adults and are able to become whatever they want in life – unique and special in their own way.

I was a deputy head and class teacher for over 22 years before studying to become a Parent Coach at The Coaching Academy, the largest Coaching Institute in Europe, and extending my training to become an NLP Master Practitioner and Trainer. I trained with Dr Richard Bandler, the co-founder of NLP in association with Paul McKenna Training and I apply my knowledge and learning to help you communicate more effectively with your kids.

Neuro-Linguistic Programming (NLP) is a bit like an 'owner's manual' for your brain. At school and college we all learnt wonderful things like history, geography and maths but we probably didn't learn how to feel good or to have great relationships. That's where NLP comes in. Described as the technology of the mind, the science of achievement and the study of success, NLP is a set of insights and skills with which you can manage your thoughts, moods and behaviours more successfully and communicate more effectively with others. For over 30 years, NLP students have observed or 'modelled' the behaviour and thinking styles of particularly successful people in business, education, sport and personal development to provide shortcuts to improved living and happier family relationships.

I'm not a 'Supernanny' or Mary Poppins and I don't tell people how to run their lives. What I can do as a Parent Coaching Expert is to help you find your own answers for your own family, to take your family relationships from where they are now to where you would like them to be. With two kids of my own, I know exactly what you're going through. As parents, we are all in the same boat of worrying, nurturing, chastising and celebrating our kids. It can be a real rollercoaster of emotions and challenges and nothing really prepares you for the enormous responsibilities. But I honestly believe that parenting needn't be full of battles, arguments, exasperation, guilt and exhaustion. Bringing up your own flesh and blood and sending them out into the world equipped to handle whatever life throws at them can be a real joy, privilege and source of deep personal fulfilment. My son has just left for university so I'm speaking from first-hand experience.

You might be reading this book because you are interested in picking up new ideas, different strategies or practical solutions to a problem or challenge that you might be faced with, or perhaps you are going through a time of change and transition, or maybe you're just curious to find out and learn some new ways of doing things. Whatever your reasons, I know that you want to do a great job or you wouldn't have bought this book. I really hope you enjoy exploring your role as a parent and that my book brings your family closer together and makes life with your kids more positive, relaxed and fun.

This book explores new ways to handle all the aspects of raising happy, confident, responsible, resilient kids, who are ready for life. I can help you to handle these changes without difficulty and begin the process with confidence. I will remind you to focus on the bigger picture and longer-term view – not just the family arguments, untidy bedroom or undone homework scenarios that most parents get stuck in – and encourage you as a parent to develop your own confidence, style and rhythm. With this book, you will feel less stressed, more energised and in control of your family life, which is absolutely vital for bringing up your kids.

I will teach you the key habits of successful parenting and encourage you to remain open-minded and flexible. When trying my techniques, strategies and practical ideas, be prepared to ask yourself different questions so that you can explore new ways of doing things. By having a go at the exercises throughout this book you will be able to unlock your confidence and explore your parenting potential. The key thing to remember is this: 'What you practise, you become' – so it's like learning anything; it just takes a bit of practice to make something new into a natural habit.

I will show you:

- How to identify your own parenting goals
- How to become a more confident parent
- Simple ways to communicate with your kids more successfully
- The secret to well-behaved kids while remaining calm, confident and in control at all times
- Quick and easy ways to develop your child's self-esteem
- Tried and tested strategies to cope with home/life issues

How to Get the Most from this Book

I've written this book from an interactive Parent Coaching perspective, which means I often ask open-ended questions to get you to think about your own family, and to make decisions based on your own situations and experiences. Take your time to ponder, reflect and answer the questions from your own point of view. It is not meant to be prescriptive but more a new and very different approach to looking at your relationships and hopefully offering you fresh and varied strategies for dealing with them. At times I offer you advice based on widely acknowledged, universally agreed parenting skills that are regarded as good practice, but I also offer my own experience as a teacher and parent.

As you go through the book, I will ask you from time to time to make notes on your thoughts and ideas. You can work through these exercises on your own, or you can enjoy going through the book with your partner, comparing notes and discussing what you discover. You may find, then, that your kids can't play you off against each other, as you will both be singing from the same song sheet!

You can read the book in any order – feel free to make it as personally relevant to you and your family as you want – though I recommend that you first read Chapter 1: Parenting With a Purpose, as it gives you an overview and identifies the ultimate destination of your parenting journey, so is therefore a good base on which to build.

Parenting can often feel quite overwhelming so don't try to make too many drastic changes all at the same time – relax and have fun. Your job of raising happy, confident kids is a REALLY important one!

What Is a Parent?

Being a parent is probably the most challenging and exhausting thing you will ever do in your whole life. But it is also the most rewarding, fulfilling and important job you will ever do. The highs and lows, laughter, tears, memories and moments will take your breath away – it's an adventure!

Being a parent means many things – you are a teacher, nurse, manager, taxi driver, cake maker, cleaner, counsellor, mentor and policeman all rolled into one while trying to create a happy, safe, nurturing environment for your children as they grow from toddlers to teens. So it's not always easy, and you'll find that you need different skills, techniques and strategies for each age and stage. You'll also need to be a vitally important role model in all that you do and say, and in how you behave, as your children watch, listen and learn from you, as well as being dependent on you for their total well-being, particularly when they are very young.

So let's face it, being a parent is not easy – in fact it's tough. How many people do you know who are completely confident in their parenting?

As you know, communicating with your children, whatever their age, and instilling discipline is an uphill struggle and you've probably experienced those stress-filled days of wondering if you're ever going to crack this parenting business. Maybe you have tried different approaches but are daunted by the sheer enormity of the task. Parenting in the 21st century is very different from 50 years ago as we have to protect our children from internet bullying, ever-expanding uses of technology and the pervasive influence of the media. Despite all of this, I believe you can become the expert on your child and what they need to grow into happy, healthy, confident, independent, well-balanced adults who are responsible, resilient and ready for life.

Before we begin together, here are a few basic assumptions about you:

- I believe that you love your children and want the best for them.
- I believe that you are curious and open-minded about exploring new ways to parent your kids.
- I believe that all the resources and answers you need for your family are already within you.
- I believe that you want to find better ways to communicate with your kids.
- I believe that you are willing to 'have a go' at new ways of doing things.
- I believe that you realise there is no 'right' or 'wrong' way to bring up kids and no 'perfect' parent – just personal choices.
- I believe that you accept there is no such thing as being a failure – there's only learning and feedback. Everyone makes mistakes and has setbacks – it's what you learn from these experiences that's the most important part.

Loving your child, with no strings attached, is the most important thing you can do for them and that's why it's called unconditional love. But you'll also have to make a huge number of decisions about the best way to bring up your child and that can be challenging and stressful. The choices and decisions are enormous and range from selecting their nursery and school, deciding what they eat and who they play with, to nurturing their love of sport, encouraging them to learn to play a musical instrument or choosing whether to enrol them in Brownies or Judo. This responsibility brings joy and excitement, but it can also be overwhelming, frustrating or, dare I say it, even boring at times. Most people manage these emotional and practical challenges with a mixture of love, help from relatives and friends, good advice, common sense and luck. But because most of us no longer live next door to our parents or grandparents, it's difficult to get the support, advice or listening ear that previous generations of parents easily received.

So I am here to empower you, challenge you and develop your confidence, and to enable you to turn into a positive and relaxed parent so that you can become the best that you can be.

> **You are the most important person in your child's life.**

Look at Yourself First

In this book I will be looking at different ways to raise **your** confidence as I believe it is very important for you to have a positive, relaxed and confident mindset FIRST, so that you pass that energy, vibe and family-focused approach down to your children. Raising confident children begins with you, as confidence is contagious. Throughout this book I will support, encourage and believe in you because I know first-hand how difficult and demanding bringing up children really is.

> **I believe that positive parents = confident kids!**

Handling children of any age is often a difficult experience but there are ways to remain centred, calm and in control of your own emotions, even when the world seems to be spinning faster than usual. I believe that success and happiness are not just accidents that happen to some people and not others – I believe that they are predicable results created by deliberate ways of thinking and acting. I think it helps to remember that the changes that really matter are often the smallest changes that you make. It's about becoming clear in what you want and how you pass that message on to your kids.

For years, people thought that a human being couldn't run a mile in under 4 minutes – then something amazing happened. Roger Bannister did the impossible – he ran a mile in 3 minutes 59.4 seconds, on 6 May 1954, and the world stood back in amazement and awe. But for me, the most interesting thing happened next – more and more people started to run a mile in less than 4 minutes when it had previously been thought impossible.

So what made the difference?

The perception had changed as to what was possible in the world.

Perhaps you have got stuck in believing that you are a poor parent or that you can't discipline your kids? Yet with a simple shift in **your** perception you **can** make some simple, small and easy changes that will make a big difference in your family life, your parenting confidence and your children's self-esteem. The world is a very fast-paced, hectic and frenetic place, and things are forever changing at a greater speed than in past generations. You may feel that you aren't 'doing it properly' or aren't 'getting it right' according to the experts – but parent coaching isn't like that.

I believe that you can get it right and, as I said right at the start, I also believe that the answers lie within you. You know your own children better than anyone, you love them completely and know deep down what's right for them and what's right for you. So it's not for me to tell you how to do it – it's about me asking you the right questions to help you find your own answers. It's about me giving you confidence in your own ability as a parent. By even buying this book you have done a remarkable thing – you have invested your time and money in learning and exploring a key skill that sets you apart from 98 per cent of people who spend more time learning how to work their new DVD player or washing machine than exploring their parenting skills.

Together we are going to help you handle your family life more effectively so that you can be happier, more confident, relaxed and at ease.

1

Parenting With a Purpose

Let's face it, kids are a challenge and so is the job of being a parent
– and it can catch you by surprise when it doesn't all go according
to plan. Being a parent can be truly wonderful, but it can also be
very stressful.

Before we begin on our journey together I want you to imagine that you've hired me to be your very own personal Parent
Coach. And, just like when I work with parents, I really want to
make sure that you get the best out of our time together. I want
you to enjoy doing the exercises in this book and learning about
new and different ways to parent. I want to offer you new ideas
and ways of looking at things, and practical solutions to everyday
problems that we all face as parents.

Successful parents stretch themselves, and they are curious to
see how great they can become. They keep their eyes firmly fixed
on the destination of their parenting, which is to bring up their
kids to become well-balanced, independent adults and they work
out what values and principles are important to them, so that they
can pass these on to their children.

I believe that you can tap into your own intuition as a parent
as well as feeling confident to pick up a book for advice from time
to time. There really is no shame or embarrassment in holding up
your hands and saying that you need a bit of help or inspiration
now and again.

I find it amazing that a new washing machine comes with an instruction book in five different languages, but as you walk out of the hospital with the most important bundle of your life in your arms, there are no manuals or handouts to help you. But I want you to know that no book has all the answers and that there really is no perfect parent – they only exist in Hollywood films – and it's not true that 'one size fits all', like those socks you buy at Christmas from the £1 shop.

I believe that we are all different and have our own way of bringing up our kids and no one way is necessarily better than another, but there are some basic values that we all share and this book will ask you unusual questions to get you reflecting and pondering on the bigger picture of your parenting, offering you fresh and new strategies, techniques and practical ideas to empower you with the confidence you need to raise happy, healthy and hopeful children ready to fulfil their true unlimited potential.

Let's start with an exercise that highlights the enormous amount of different things you do as a parent and how important your job really is. This exercise helps you to appreciate just how many different roles you play, and how wide the amount of different skills you need to raise a happy, confident child – emotionally, physically, socially, spiritually and practically.

Write a job description for being a parent

- What are the hours?
- How many days per week?
- How many years?
- What is the pay?
- What training do you get?
- What jobs do you have to do?
- What skills do you need?

Take some time to write down the answers to these questions. Then, consider what your job description for your role as a parent would be in one sentence.

What have you learnt or discovered about your role as a parent from doing this exercise?

Were you surprised by the different roles you play? Perhaps you were surprised by the different skills you need to master as a parent. You're the managing director of the most important company in the world – your family. You are juggling and dealing with everything that raising a family throws at you, from negotiating, organising, budgeting and crisis-management, to meeting deadlines, instilling discipline, nurturing self-esteem and multi-tasking.

As parents, we are generally very good at talking ourselves down and we tend to focus on what we get 'wrong' rather than what we get 'right'. Most parents I work with beat themselves up about what they 'can't do', 'haven't done', 'should do' or 'could do better' but the exercise is designed to help you focus on the enormously wide range of skills you need to learn as a parent, and most of which you probably already practise without even knowing it.

On the day my son left home to start university, I wrote this rather tongue-in-cheek blog post, to show that most parents underestimate the wide-ranging tasks a parent has to learn as they go along.

The Toughest Job in the World

Job Description
A long-term player needed for challenging, permanent work in an often exhausting, tiring and overwhelming environment. Candidates must possess excellent communication and organisational skills and be

willing to work all day from very early morning, evenings, weekends and frequent 24-hour shifts or late into the night with interrupted sleep. You will need negotiation skills, excellent time-management skills as well as the ability to knock up a model out of papier mâché and an electric battery at very short notice, to say nothing of baking cakes for the school fête, managing a budget, painting rainbows, singing songs late into the night to get your offspring to sleep, and playing endless rounds of Snakes and Ladders. There are often countless sports matches to attend on Sunday mornings in the freezing cold, music recitals and swimming galas. Unfortunately travel expenses are not reimbursed.

Responsibilities

You must realise that you will keep this job for the rest of your life and have the enormous responsibility for bringing up happy, confident, well-balanced, independent, well-rounded and emotionally balanced adults. You will also have to be prepared to be hated, at least temporarily, for saying 'no' to too many sweets before dinner, for insisting that they go to bed on time, for getting them off the computer before they've finished their very important game and for insisting they come home from parties at a reasonable hour!

You must be willing to bite your tongue repeatedly as well as accept that you will be indispensable one minute and an embarrassment the next.

Advancement and Promotion

There is no possibility of either. Your job is to remain in the same position for years, without complaining, constantly retraining and updating your skills so that your offspring can ultimately surpass you and leave you to fly the nest without so much as a 'thank you' at the end of the adventure.

Previous Experience

None required, but on-the-job training is offered on a continually exhausting basis where you make it up most of the time and hope that it'll all turn out all right in the end!

Wages

None, as this is a labour of love. In fact, you must pay your offspring, offering frequent raises and bonuses, incentives and rewards both emotionally and financially. A balloon payment is due when they turn 18 and attend college, and when they marry you usually contribute an enormous amount of your savings to their 'special day'. When you die, you give them whatever income you have left.

Benefits

There is no pension, no tuition reimbursement, no paid holidays and no stock options. However, the job offers limitless opportunities for personal growth and free hugs, cuddles, laughter, joy and memories that will last your whole life and the adventure will be the most rewarding and fulfilling job of your entire life.

How You Rate Yourself as a Parent

In order to be the best parent you can be, you need to pat yourself on the back from time to time. You need to recognise what you do well because what you say about yourself has tremendous power and influence on your confidence. If you are upbeat, positive and value your role as a parent, then you will be providing a positive model for your children. Let's focus on your qualities and strengths as proof that you have what it takes to be a great parent.

Take your time and really ponder and reflect on these questions, writing down your answers if it helps:

- What are your three most significant achievements as a parent?
- What is the greatest challenge that you have overcome as a parent?
- What are the three things you love most about being a parent?
- What personal qualities and skills make you a good parent? (For example being good at problem-solving, being patient and being a good listener.)
- What things do you love most about your children?
- How has having children changed your life for the better?

The challenge in the questions above is to focus on what you've come through, or learnt, and to nurture yourself by recognising and celebrating the wonderfully diverse roles you play throughout the lifetime of your children.

The Principles of Good Parenting

It's true that the basic principles of good parenting apply to all children and stay the same throughout childhood and adolescence, but the way these principles are put into practice must be tailored to fit your child's age, personality, interests and circumstances. As your child grows and matures, their abilities, concerns and needs change too. Good parenting is flexible, so while you shouldn't change any of the fundamentals, you must adapt them to fit your child's character and stage of development, and your family style.

The important thing to remember is that your role as a parent changes as your child grows. It's that simple.

What worked well when your child was in nursery won't necessarily work when they reach junior school, nor will it likely work when they enter adolescence. You can't talk to your 11-year-old the same way as you spoke to your 4-year-old. This may seem obvious, but you'd be surprised at how many parents refuse to change their ways as their children develop and then find themselves wondering why they are having so much difficulty using techniques that always seemed to work before.

I think it is helpful to understand what developments are taking place and what they mean to you as a parent. There are four very important points to bear in mind.

Inner growth

When your child develops from one stage to the next, they are changing on the inside as well as on the outside. Your child is not just growing in shoe size but is changing in the way they think and feel: what they think about themselves, what they are capable of and how they relate to other people, including you.

Stages of development

The psychological stages of development that children go through are reasonably predictable, which makes it easier to anticipate. The strange thing is that most parents make a special effort to learn how to parent during infancy, but they don't expend as much energy on the pre-school, pre-teen or adolescent stages and just hope that problems will go away.

Don't make that mistake. Learn about each stage of development before your child gets there so that you can remain prepared and flexible to the changes (see the boxed text for more information). This is a key skill in being a good parent and building self-confident, well-balanced children.

Every child is unique

Remember that children are all individuals and develop at their own pace and speed and you can't rush them through a particular phase. Sometimes they take two steps forward and three steps back!

Grow together

Your children are developing and changing, therefore so are you! Enjoy the opportunities being presented to you and don't see them as a negative experience. Grow, develop and discover together. Just bear in mind that the drive and independence that is making your three-year-old say 'no' all the time is actually the same process that makes your thirteen-year-old daughter argumentative at the dinner table. It is also what makes her more inquisitive in the classroom.

Child Development

All parents worry about how well their children are developing. Are they talking enough? Should they be reading more? Are they growing? Are they learning new concepts at the appropriate time for their age?

Areas of Development
Children develop skills in five main areas:

---

1. Cognitive Development

This is the child's ability to learn and solve problems. For example, this includes a two-month-old baby learning to explore the environment with their hands or eyes or a five-year-old learning how to read.

2. Social and Emotional Development

This is your child's ability to interact socially with others, doing some things for themselves and learning self-control. Examples of this type of development would include: a six-week-old baby smiling, a ten-month-old baby waving goodbye, or a six-year-old knowing how to take turns in games at school.

3. Speech and Language Development

This is your child's ability to both understand and use language. For example, this includes a twelve-month-old baby saying their first words, a two-year-old naming parts of their body, or a four-year-old learning to say 'feet' instead of 'foots'.

4. Fine Motor Skill Development

This is your child's ability to use their small muscles, specifically their hands and fingers to pick up small objects, hold a knife and fork, turn pages in a book, use a pencil to draw, learn to sew, manipulate their school tie, do up their shoelaces, or throw and catch a ball. It's about developing their dexterity.

5. Gross Motor Skill Development

This is your child's ability to use their larger muscles. For example, a six-month-old baby learns how to sit up with some support, a twelve-month-old baby learns to pull up to standing by holding on to furniture, and a seven-year-old learns to skip or swim.

Stages of Development

Age 1

Most parents see their child's first birthday as an important milestone as it marks the transition from baby to toddler. Your child will go through a period of rapid development in the 12 months between their first and second birthdays – and parents usually can't wait for their little one to learn to walk and talk. But remember that children develop at their own pace, and it's not a race or a competition, so try not to compare your child with others.

Age 2

Most parents dread the 'terrible twos' and worry about how they will deal with the tantrums that often begin before their child's second birthday. It can be hard to adjust to your child's dramatic mood swings, so they need you to relax and stay centred and positive, as they strive for independence. They are going through a period of physical and emotional change.

Age 3

After their third birthday, you will notice that your child is becoming increasingly independent. As they try to make sense of the world around them you will be asked lots of questions that usually start with 'Why?' They will also begin to develop a sense of right and wrong, and will be keen to gain your praise and approval.

Age 4

Many children start school when they are four, which is an important milestone for them and for you. Some children are very excited about going to school, whereas some are rather nervous. Just give your child lots of reassurance and focus on how much fun they will have and perhaps begin the basics of reading and writing before they start, to give them confidence.

Age 5

At the age of five, children become much more confident in all areas of their social, emotional and physical development and your child will be keen to show off their achievements – so it's important to show interest in their schoolwork and find a place to display their artwork, swimming certificates, stickers and rewards from school.

Ages 6–8

Between the ages of six and eight, you will notice that your child becomes noticeably more independent and their friends become very important to them. They respond well to simple, clear guidelines, rules and expectations that apply to everyone in your house.

Ages 9–12

Many parents are unprepared for the changes their child will face between the ages of nine and twelve. So don't be surprised if your nine-year-old becomes curious about their body or may even begin puberty. Most children change schools at the age of eleven or twelve, which can be another milestone in their development, as they leave the familiar comfort zone of their junior school and enter the bigger, more unfamiliar environment of secondary school, where they begin to mix with older pupils and will experience more demands on them to become independent by their new teachers.

The Destination of Your Parenting

I believe that the key to successful parenting is having a sense of direction and a clear vision of your destination. When I was on my first NLP Practitioner course, I got chatting to a pilot who told me something that really surprised me: the majority of the time an aeroplane doesn't travel on its specific flight course – it's actually off course for 90 per cent of its journey!

I wondered how planes reach their destination, when there are so many factors such as air currents and weather constantly moving them off course. Obviously, the pilot's navigation instruments, skill and expertise help to bring the aeroplane to its safe destination, and throughout the flight the pilot is constantly guiding and adjusting the plane towards its intended flight path. But the key thing for me was that the ultimate destination is always in the pilot's mind throughout the journey, and no matter how far away from its route the plane is flying, he is constantly steering it back towards the intended landing place. This made me think that bringing up children is not so dissimilar to piloting a plane – and most of us don't even have a flight plan!

It is impossible to be a perfect parent all the time and it's difficult staying on a really tight, defined course because there are too many variables, such as your children's personalities, the pressures of work, other kids in the family, looking after elderly relatives and all the other unexpected dynamics and challenges of everyday living. I believe that good families – even great families – are off track 90 per cent of the time, just like aircraft. But effective and successful parents do have a flight plan. They know where they are going and what they want to achieve – they have a strategy, not necessarily a specific, hard-and-fast map that's cast in stone, but an overall plan to guide them to their destination.

By designing and planning an appropriate parenting path in your mind, you too can keep yourself from straying too far off course, and it will really help you to reach your parenting goals.

Think about where you are going in your parenting and where you want to end up. Every family is individual with its own way of doing things and its own rhythm, but sitting down together and talking about where you all want to go focuses you on the destination and makes being a family exciting – a bit like planning a holiday.

'The wonderful thing is that vision is greater than baggage.'
~ Stephen Covey

So let's design your family's flight plan so that you can have a safe and enjoyable trip and not just fly by the seat of your pants! We'll start by learning what's important to your family.

What's your family all about?

All families face difficult pressures and stressful times. When people lead busy lives, they often take their frustrations, tiredness or worries out on each other when they get home at the end of a hectic day. But if you are aware that this can happen and make the effort to step back from a situation when it becomes stressful, you can learn how to stay strong, happy and supportive of each other.

Take a few minutes to write down all the things you believe are important in a family – things like respecting each other's ideas, thoughts and opinions; respecting someone else's belongings; being patient and taking care of younger children; showing tolerance, kindness and patience towards others; being helpful; working hard at school; showing tenacity; being curious or conscientious; being dependable and reliable; being adaptable; being generous and fun loving; or being thoughtful. Just write all the things that you believe are important principles in life, and in family life in particular.

What makes some families strong and what is their flight plan?

I believe the strength of a family comes from your inner beliefs and values – from the parent, as you are the one flying the plane. If you know what you are trying to achieve, then in the long run you will succeed and you won't be blown so easily off course. Take a few moments here to ponder and reflect on what you are trying to achieve as a parent in the long term, as it will give you enormous clarity and confidence, and a clear vision of where you are trying to get to with your family.

I remember reading the amazing autobiography of Lance Armstrong, an American former-professional road-racing cyclist, who won the Tour de France a record seven consecutive times, after having survived testicular cancer, and it got me thinking about his competitive spirit, his driving force, his resilience, his attitude and his mindset in life. What makes him special? What makes him different? What made him get back up to have another go and not be beaten by a traumatic diagnosis? I think it's about having a goal, having a vision, having a passion and a purpose; he knew where he wanted to get to and what he wanted to achieve.

So how do you create this powerful mindset and attitude in your family?

Begin with the end in mind

Most parents are not accustomed to looking at the bigger, long-term picture of their parenting. Most families just muddle along, reacting to life's circumstances as they come up. But as a Parent Coach I'm here to get you to think and act differently to the 98 per cent of other parents.

In my workshops I always get parents to think about the long-term goals of their parenting. We start by looking at their family ethos, philosophy and values. Creating your own family ethos or philosophy keeps you firmly focused and can serve you like a compass when your family strays off course from time to time. Your family ethos keeps your destination clear.

Take some time now and turn off your mobile phone, turn off the TV or grab a cup of coffee so that you can ponder and reflect on what's really important to you as a parent and as a person. This is what I call beginning with the end in mind.

What values are important to you?

Relax and ask yourself these simple questions:

- What is the purpose of our family?
- What kind of family do we want to be?
- What kinds of things do we want to do?
- What kinds of feelings do we want to have in our home?
- How would a stranger describe the atmosphere in our home?
- What kinds of relationships do we want to have with each other?
- What things are truly important to us as a family?
- What do we stand for?

In other words – what are the values of your family?

These are very important and rather unusual questions to ask yourself but the reason for doing this is that your values are like your personal compass – they guide your decisions. They are what you stand for and most people or parents don't spend any time actually analysing this, but if you're not absolutely clear about your values, how can you possibly pass them on to your children? Values are the things by which you live your life and on which you are not willing to compromise. They drive all your behaviours and it's because of your values that you do something and decide afterwards whether it was good or bad or sits comfortably with you. Examples of a value are being honest, having determination, being kind and compassionate towards others, having the ability to finish a task, doing well at school, always doing your best, always telling the truth, being loyal, being trustworthy, being considerate, etc.

Write down all your guiding values by which you live your life so that you can see really clearly what they are, and take a few moments to reflect on who gave you these values. Was it your parents, teachers, aunts, uncles, friends, your authority figures, your religious leaders? Are those the values you choose to hold now and want to pass on to your children? If you discover that you don't like what you have revealed, only reflect on the values that you **do** want to pass on to your children.

I bet you've never done this type of exercise before, because most parents don't actually stop to ponder the bigger picture of their parenting, but I think considering your values really helps to give you clarity, direction and focus.

It's also a great idea to get your partner to do the same thing so that you can see if you are both going in the same direction. If you find that you're not, don't panic. Have a coffee together, or maybe even go out for a glass of wine to chat over what's important to you as a couple, as it's really important for your kids to know and be clear about what your values are as a family unit. Take some time to define what you feel is important to your family. It's rather like having a mission statement – what you stand for, what your family is all about and the principles that you choose to govern your family life and that you feel are important to you all. It's all part of planning your parenting destination and deciding what kind of family you want to be.

Also consider if there are any areas of your lifestyle that you'd like to change. Would you like to spend more time playing together, riding bikes on Saturdays or eating together more during the week, or would you like to create more personal family traditions or enjoy getting home from the office a little earlier once a week to read a story together at bedtime?

Think of some small changes that you could make simply and easily this week and stick to them because you will then be committing to the sort of family life you want to create. It will help you to feel more in control of your relationships; like you not only have a map, but also a compass. Consciously deciding on the things you'd like to change will give you a clear, shared vision of the destination you want to reach as a family.

Practise what you preach

Think about how you pass on your values – how do you pass them on in your words, in your actions or in the way you talk to your kids? Do you talk about being patient and tolerant but scream at the driver who cuts you up at the roundabout? Your children will remember how you act far more than what you say, so be careful and mindful to walk your talk.

Sharing your family values

The next thing to do is to decide a time when you can all sit down round the kitchen table without the TV on and have a talk about the 'spirit' or philosophy of your family and start planning it together, with your kids involved too. Even young children have clear ideas about what a happy family looks, sounds and feels like so include them in your family time and listen to what they say – children's innocence always catches you by surprise in its simplicity and truth.

The secret is to make the conversation fun and enjoyable and think ahead so that you have an idea of what you want to talk about with your children and some simple ways to include them in the discussion. A really helpful technique I use with my clients is to plan what you are going to say and how you are going to say it in your mind beforehand. Sit quietly and imagine what you'll see: the kids wondering what's happening and fidgeting; what you'll hear: maybe giggling and laughing; and how you'll feel when you are in control and preparing something new and important to you.

It's probably not a good idea to introduce this idea when you are exhausted, angry, tired or in the middle of a family upheaval. A good time is when you are on holiday and are all feeling relaxed and chilled out or simply choose a time when you are at ease and feeling positive, upbeat and ready to chat about the 'spirit' of your family. Just take your time, be patient and don't rush it.

What's Important to You as a Parent?

Here are some more questions to ponder to help you get clear about what's important to you as a parent:

- How do you develop, nurture and grow your child's self-esteem? (Do you focus on what they get right, more than what they get wrong? Do you consistently speak positively to them; praise what you like to see so that you get more of that behaviour? Do you talk, laugh and joke with them? Do you spend time together doing fun activities? Do you eat together, read together? Relax together?)

- How do you develop good habits such as being on time, eating healthily, exercising, having good personal hygiene, showing tenacity, keeping their word, telling the truth, passing exams, doing their homework, being kind, helping others, being kind to their siblings or giving back to the community?

- Does your child get enough sleep so that they can get up on time and without being grumpy and function effectively at school? What time would be sensible and realistic for your child to go to bed? How can you encourage your child to take responsibility for getting enough sleep?

- What are your views on going to play on weeknights or your rules about sleepovers?

- What are your expectations and routines about homework, tidying up, helping around the house? How do you encourage your children with these tasks?

- What are your views or rules about mobile-phone use?

- What is a balanced amount of TV/DVD/computer games to watch or play each day/week? How can you encourage responsibility in those areas? What things can you do to encourage balance, commitment and honesty?

- What are your views on education, schoolwork and passing exams?

- How can you actively and positively support, encourage and remain interested in what your children are doing at school?

- How can you help, support and encourage your children to set simple goals and achieve them?
- How do you help them manage money?
- How do you encourage them to show respect to others, other people's property and younger and older members of the family and community at large?
- How do you show an interest in the films they watch, games they play, music they like and things that make them laugh?
- How do you spend time together? What new ways could you find to spend time with them?

These questions give you clarity about what's important to you and although I'm suggesting you remain flexible, centred, grounded and mature in your approach it's about choosing your battles so that your kids feel you care but they also know that there are some simple boundaries and rules.

Where Does Your Parenting Style Come From?

Raising children often brings up issues for parents about their past. Some of the parents I work with don't want to repeat the patterns of their past, others fall into the same patterns and others just don't think about these aspects at all. But it will help your confidence if you are aware of how the way you were brought up has influenced you now as a parent so you can either carry on, or change some aspects of what you are currently repeating.

Reflect and think about some of the important messages you received from your parents – both your mother and your father – and what you learnt about yourself from school experiences and from other important authority figures in your life, such as your teachers, religious figures, older family members or other close adults. Are those beliefs empowering and positive, or disempowering and negative? You may discover some aspects to yourself that surprise, delight or shock you and, as you reflect on the messages you received, consider whether those beliefs you hold about yourself are true now. Were they ever true and, if you don't like what you have discovered, what would you like to change from today onwards about the messages you received? I hope you can now see the very important role you play in shaping the messages and beliefs your children pick up from you, both consciously and unconsciously.

How do you see yourself as parent? Choose one belief that you'd like to change about yourself as a parent and write it down. For example: I'm not patient enough, I shout too much, I don't play with my kids enough...

Now ask yourself:

- What would I have to believe in order to change this view of myself and to see how this belief is ridiculous, absurd or untrue?
- Where did I get this belief about myself and what will holding on to this belief cost me emotionally if I don't let go of it?
- What will it ultimately cost me and my family relationships if I don't let go of this belief?

Take some time now to rephrase the belief you had about yourself. For example if you said: 'I can never succeed as a good parent because I'm hopeless at discipline because my parents were too strict with me and I don't want to inflict that kind of harsh style of discipline on my kids,' this could be rephrased into: 'Because my parents were too strict with me, I'm a more balanced parent with more consistent, flexible but fair boundaries that suit my family.'

Being conscious of how you are thinking about yourself as a parent is one of the most essential skills you can develop so take some time to write out your current beliefs about yourself, and if they don't feel good, reframe them into something more positive.

Changing your critical, negative beliefs about yourself makes you feel more confident, more in control, more focused on getting a better result, and it helps you to look forward more positively, releasing you from being too judgemental about yourself. If you have a positive outlook you can move forward as a parent; if you are negative, you will stay stuck.

The Relationship You Want with Your Children

All families are strengthened by the expressions of caring, appreciation and love that everyone shows towards each other and members of strong families always find ways to support and encourage each other even when someone makes a mistake or gets it wrong. They make decisions, solve family problems and do things together and they have the mindset that everyone participates and everyone joins in.

The things you say and do with your children determine the kind of relationship you have with them, and sometimes after some reflection and standing back, you may realise that the relationships with your children may need to change.

Often relationships with children centre too much on control and correction, with parents trying to get the children to do things the children don't want to do, or trying to stop their children from doing things they want to do. For example, have you ever tried to force a struggling child into a car seat on a wet Tuesday at the supermarket? Have you ever tried to stop your kids from eating chocolate or crisps before dinner? Have you tried to get your children to do their homework, eat their vegetables or stop fighting with each other? Then you'll know how hard it is to get children to do as they are told!

Naturally, parents generally have more power and authority than children, as we are bigger and stronger. But it's hard to force people to do something they don't want to do. Sometimes we find ourselves spending all of our time shouting, nagging and moaning at our kids, trying to bribe, convince or force them into doing something that we want them to do. That's the trouble with control: it takes over the relationship. It can be the only thing that you and your children seem to talk about, so it's not a very good basis for a balanced and healthy relationship or even a loving and fun one.

If your relationship with your children is based purely on correction it can become a bit strained and sometimes even insulting. I've heard people in supermarkets saying things like, 'How can you be so stupid?' or 'Can't you do anything right?' These types of insults are really damaging as they don't give children useful information. They only make them feel bad. Even if you avoid insults, too much correction can still be bad for your relationship because there are better, more fun and more interesting things to talk about.

I'm not saying control and correction is always bad – of course it's a necessary and essential part of raising your children – but when control and correction are all that a child gets from you, your child can become discouraged or even rebellious; so really think about the sort of relationship you want to create in the long term and don't let controlling and correcting your children be the only thing you focus on in your relationship.

Most of us spend a lot of time talking about only a few things with our children. 'Wash your hands.' 'Stop teasing your sister.' 'Do your homework.' 'Stop that.' 'Go to bed,' which sets us up to be rather negative with our children. Stop for a moment here and think about your last week with your kids. What are the things you have talked, shouted, nagged or moaned about with each of them? Think about whether the conversations were friendly (helpful, happy) or unfriendly (angry, bossy, unkind). Go back over your week and notice and observe what you saw, what you heard, what you said and how you felt in different scenarios.

Now step into the shoes of your kids and see the previous week from their perspective – really seeing the situations from their eyes, their ears and their feelings. What do you discover?

Now step into the shoes of your partner, really imagining what your family looks, sounds and feels like from their point of view. What do you discover?

This is quite a powerful thing to do, isn't it? Don't panic or feel guilty if you don't like what you see – this is why you are reading this book: to help you make small changes that can make a big difference in everyone's life. So relax and think of just one or two small changes you could make this week to behave differently – in your words, actions or tone of voice – and try them out and see what happens.

The Pause Button Exercise

I teach all my clients this really simple but very effective technique.

1. Imagine a situation that's all going a bit pear-shaped and not as you planned or expected. You're tired, the kids are tired or hungry, and you are feeling overwhelmed, exhausted, weary or just plain fed up repeating yourself over and over again. You can feel your anger, frustration or temper beginning to rise…

2. So, instead, just imagine that you are holding your DVD or TV remote control in your hand. Now press 'PAUSE' on it while you take a deep breath and freeze-frame where you are for a split second. This detaches you from your immediate situation and helps you to disassociate yourself from it while you ask yourself better questions.

3. Now ask:

'What is it I want to happen?'

'What is it I want the kids to do?'

'What is it I want to say?'

'How do I want to say it?'

4. Relax and bring yourself gently back into the present.

This technique helps you to feel back in control of the situation again and helps you to relax and feel more confident, knowing that you are not simply being a reactive parent but a proactive, aware parent. It gives you breathing space for a couple of minutes and is a really simple but highly effective tool in your parenting toolkit.

How you treat one another

I am a very positive and enthusiastic person by nature and hopefully that rubs off on my parenting. In order to make your relationships with your children more positive, think about what you want the relationships to be like.

- Would you like to have more fun time with each child?
- Would you like to nag less often?
- Would you like to share your hobby or passion with them?
- Would you like to spend more time chatting to them?

- Would you like to spend more time reading them stories?
- Would you like to laugh and joke together more?

Think about the ways in which you can achieve these things:

- How could you build more opportunities for doing what you'd like to do more of?
- How could you build more affection into your relationships and remove some of the control and correction?
- How could you show more respect to each other?

We expect adults to be individuals and to have different likes and dislikes, sometimes different to ours, and to be good at some things and not at others. But it often surprises us that our kids are also individuals with their own tastes, styles and abilities. All children have different rates of development and different personalities. Knowing this can help you to be more patient and understanding towards your kids. Show them that you really care about them by accepting each of them as individuals and think about how you treat one another in the words you use or the way you say things. Remember that you are a huge role model and watching the way you do things is the way your kids learn, so relax and be a respectful, positive parent.

The Atmosphere in Your Home

Reflecting on the atmosphere in your home can act like a thermostat and marker for the way your children see their surroundings and can be a very effective way of noticing what's currently going on in your house.

Take a moment to consider whether you are a Thermometer or a Thermostat. A thermometer tells you when something isn't right; it's an indicator that something's out of sync, unbalanced, out of kilter, ill, broken, troubled or in need of help. Whereas a thermostat brings everything back into balance. This is far more valuable, as it manages to keep a family environment in sync with what's going on, as it bends not breaks through change, it adapts, it's flexible and it keeps adjusting to meet the needs of a growing, maturing family.

Have a think now and jot down your first thoughts about the atmosphere in your home so that you can tweak your family thermostat. Is it relaxed, frenetic, chaotic, noisy, tense, happy, a place to feel at ease, a place to laugh, bring home friends and to feel safe? If you are not completely happy with your answer have a think about some changes you could make to improve it this week.

- What makes it frenetic? Is it the dog rushing madly about barking? Then put him in the utility room for a bit. Is it the kids running about playing Harry Potter? Then send them outside to play.
- Is it chaotic because you aren't good at organising time? Then just take some time to sit down and plan out your day without leaving it all to the last minute.
- Is it tense because you are feeling stressed and overwhelmed? Then think of simple ways to delegate some of your chores and jobs around the house.

Also ask your family their thoughts on the atmosphere in your home. Get everyone involved in finding the solutions and thinking of new and different ways to improve the atmosphere if there are areas that your family don't like. Then talk about the ideas together and see what answers you can come up with and can agree to.

Positive and negative anchors

What are the triggers that affect your moods at home? Pause for a moment to ponder this rather unusual question as it could be running a pattern in your house that may not be very empowering or useful.

Here's an example of a positive anchor that helps you to relax, feel good and enjoy your home life. Imagine the smell of a log fire on a relaxing winter Sunday afternoon after a lovely lunch and a good glass of red wine. This is a positive anchor as it brings back happy, soothing memories that affect your mood in a positive way.

Now imagine the sound of the TV blaring, empty crisp packets on the floor, shoes and socks scattered all over the living room, the curtains not drawn and your children slumped in front of the TV, when you first walk in tired from work. This scenario immediately kick-starts your stress and unhappiness so it is a negative anchor.

By recognising your different experiences you can start changing your negative anchors into positive experiences. Take a few minutes now to ponder and reflect on the positive and negative anchors that trigger you, either into a good mood or into a bad mood. This is not intended to make you beat yourself up, but to empower you to notice the triggers so that you can make small changes and feel far more in control of your family life, which will really improve your confidence. Be curious and inquisitive to learn what your anchors are, so that you can change them for the better. It's a lot easier to blame someone else for your bad luck, unhappy life or bad day, but then you are playing the victim and not taking responsibility for your attitude and approach to your circumstances. Take control of your attitude, take control of the situation you find yourself in, take control of your stress levels and learn to feel more empowered and confident!

So ask yourself what negative feelings you have and then have fun changing your attitude and approach whenever you notice yourself falling into this pattern – swap your images around, relax and get back in control. So now the sound of the TV blaring, empty crisp packets on the floor, shoes and socks scattered all over the living room, the curtains not drawn and your children slumped in front of the TV when you first walk in tired from work is an opportunity to teach your kids about your house rules: about putting things in the bin, putting socks and shoes in the basket by the door and having the TV on at a certain time each day at a certain level of sound.

It's also about you recognising your trigger – relaxing, even smiling and saying to yourself, 'Ah here's an opportunity to teach the kids what I DO want.' It's not always easy the first or second time you do this but it is really worthwhile, and this simple re-frame can really help to change your mood, your attitude and your approach to life's challenges as it helps you to feel more in control of your life, which can only be a great thing.

The Ideal Parent?

Cruella de Vil or Mary Poppins? That is the question! What skills and qualities do you want to demonstrate: love, calmness, compassion, control, respect, integrity, fun, fairness? The decision is yours and yours alone as you have the power to CHOOSE your style, skills and ways of bringing up your children.

Most parents have never taken the time to ponder these types of questions, so this puts you ahead of the game in taking the first steps to becoming a great parent. I hope you have enjoyed stepping into this more unusual, more reflective, slightly detached perspective on your parenting. This is what I call 'Awareness

Parenting': These thought-provoking questions help you to detach from the mundane and humdrum, and empower you to see yourself from the point of view of your children, analysing and examining life from a completely different angle, which will make you more self-aware, discerning and a better parent, consciously choosing the way you want to bring up your children.

2

The Secret of Success: YOUR Confidence

What is confidence? Have you got it? Can you lose it? Or can you develop it? Confidence is not some miracle pill you can buy in a health-food shop, but I do believe it's like a muscle that can be built up over time with practice. At its core, confidence is the ability to take appropriate and effective action in any situation, no matter how difficult or challenging it appears to you. If you are a confident parent, you have more fun, more freedom and more opportunities to do what really works for you.

How can you tell if you are a confident parent? Here are some ways to recognise if you are:

- You generally feel centred and balanced.
- You feel relaxed in most situations with your kids.
- You are proactive rather than defensive.
- You know that you are able to handle whatever life throws at you, even if you can't control it.
- You're able to laugh at yourself and not take things too seriously.
- You know that everything will turn out okay in the end, no matter how long it takes.

So how do you feel? Confident, wobbly or a mixture of both? By doing some of the exercises in this chapter regularly you will develop and improve your confidence.

The Importance of Parenting Confidence

Self-confidence is extremely important in almost every area of our lives, yet so many people struggle to master it. It is also a very important aspect to becoming a great parent, as it sets you up to succeed in your family relationships. Confident parents speak clearly, they hold their heads high and they answer questions assuredly, and their children do as they are told more readily and feel more secure as their parents exude an air of calm authority.

Let's look at the difference between 'inner confidence' – which nobody can see or feel other than you – and 'outer confidence' – which is the level of confidence perceived by the people around you. With both, you can develop and instil an air of quiet confidence and stability.

As a parent it is your job to lay the foundation of a good balance between inner and outer confidence.

The four main elements of inner confidence

These are the vital features of inner confidence:

● **Self-love**

Self-love means feeling good enough just the way you are, approving of yourself completely, including in the presence of others, trusting yourself and treating yourself with complete respect. Confident people have self-love and they behave in a way that is self-nurturing – looking after their health and well-being; it is obvious to everyone else that they love themselves. Our subconscious minds are programmed by simple, repeated instructions and the messages that we receive from others around us, so for children to develop self-love, it is very important that they learn to enjoy being nurtured and how to do this for themselves. They need to feel proud of their good features and be encouraged to make the most of them and take responsibility for their own happiness.

- **Self-knowledge**
  People with inner confidence often reflect on their feelings, thoughts and behaviours. They can see themselves objectively, are firmly aware of their identity and comfortable as individuals. If children develop good self-knowledge, they will be more able to meet their full potential and will not be so defensive at the first hint of criticism. They are more likely to have friends who are 'open', as they know what qualities they need from friendship, and they will be able to stand up to peer pressure – a very important attribute during teenage years.

- **Clear goals**
  Confident people usually have a clear idea of why they are taking a particular course of action, and have realistically worked out the kinds of results they will get. If children learn to set themselves goals, they will have more positive energy and motivation to achieve things, will be more persistent, and will learn to monitor their own progress in the light of their goals. Even decision-making will become relatively easy for them, because they will have a clear idea of what they want and how to get it. So, teaching a child how to set simple, clear, achievable goals makes them less dependent on others to inspire them

to do things and will help them develop into a self-confident adult with a sense of purpose.

- **Positive thinking**

  Confident people expect life to go well and look for good, positive experiences. Because of this, they are usually great company. Children who learn to think positively see the best in people and believe that most problems have a solution, and they don't waste their energy worrying about possible negative outcomes. They like the excitement of growth and development, so are flexible to change and generally see the bright side of life.

The four main elements of outer confidence

It's no wonder that really great schools pay attention to the attainment of these skills, as well as academic achievements, because they know that children who have inner confidence will have a huge head start in the adult world, and that they will also stand a much better chance of having a fulfilling personal and social life.

- **Communication**

  People who are able to communicate effectively are less frustrated and more empathetic to other people. They are able to make small talk with people of all ages and all kinds of backgrounds, and they know how to move conversations from small talk to a deeper level. They use non-verbal communication effectively so that it matches their verbal language, and they read other people's body language easily. They can discuss and argue rationally and articulately, and they can speak in public without being paralysed with anxiety.

- **Assertiveness**

  If you teach your children to be assertive, they will rarely have to resort to aggression or passive tactics (i.e. shying away from saying what they really mean and using moodiness, sighing or withdrawing) to get what they want out of life or relationships. They will be able to express their needs straightforwardly and stand up for their rights and the rights of others. They will receive compliments freely and sensitively and give and receive constructive criticism easily.

- **Self-presentation**

  This skill will teach children the importance of looking the part of a confident person. It will enable them to make a good first impression. It will enable them to choose the clothes that are appropriate for different roles and occasions and it will not restrict them by trying to please others continually.

- **Emotional control**

  If feelings aren't managed well, they can get out of control. Children need to be taught how to reach a balance – to have fun, get excited, let go, and also to calm down, stay centred and relax. If children are taught this skill, they will trust themselves and won't be so unpredictable. They will be able to take on more challenges because they know they can handle their anxieties, fears and frustrations. They will learn how to grieve healthily and accept the rich tapestry of life's emotions, like sibling rivalry, jealousy, injustice and guilt. But they will also understand love and happiness, and the spontaneous 'letting your hair down' times.

Assess Your Confidence

Confidence is by its very nature difficult to measure or assess because other people normally form an opinion about how confident you are based on your outside actions, but only you know deep down how you feel on the inside. Of course, how you feel differs in different situations. You may feel really confident at work but unsure with your teenager, or you may have suffered a blow to your confidence through something like a divorce, a redundancy or a major life change.

The secret to confident parenting is to take small baby steps in the right direction and allow yourself to make mistakes. Remember that the Millennium Dome wasn't built in a day, so forgive yourself if you wobble. The secret is to stay optimistic and to focus on the bright side when you hit a setback. Treat each day as a learning experience, rather than pretending that you are an expert with nothing new to discover, and be willing to take risks.

Here is a fun quiz to assess your current parenting confidence. Completing it will give you a very simple idea of the main areas in your life that are currently affecting your confidence. Read the 20 statements below and jot down how strongly you agree or disagree with them. There are no right or wrong answers but give yourself some time to think properly about each answer. You are doing this quiz to get a snapshot of how you are feeling just at this particular moment. You can take it at any time and, if you like, take it regularly so that you can see how you change and develop.

Question	Strongly agree	Agree	Feel neutral	Disagree	Strongly Disagree
1. I have a really clear sense of what's important to me.	5	4	3	2	1
2. I know what I want to achieve in my family life.	5	4	3	2	1
3. I never beat myself up about what I do or get wrong with my kids.	5	4	3	2	1
4. I can always stand back and think clearly when things get emotional or out of hand.	5	4	3	2	1
5. I enjoy bringing up my kids.	5	4	3	2	1
6. I'm known for being optimistic in my family.	5	4	3	2	1
7. I see myself as an enthusiastic parent.	5	4	3	2	1
8. I respect myself and the people around me.	5	4	3	2	1
9. I have a clear idea of my strengths and weaknesses as a parent.	5	4	3	2	1
10. I know what others in my family see as my strengths.	5	4	3	2	1
11. I include others in the family in making decisions where it's appropriate.	5	4	3	2	1
12. I see both the bigger picture and the smaller details in family situations.	5	4	3	2	1
13. I enjoy taking on new challenges.	5	4	3	2	1
14. I embrace learning new ways to do things.	5	4	3	2	1

Question	Strongly agree	Agree	Feel neutral	Disagree	Strongly Disagree
15. I'm able to handle stress easily.	5	4	3	2	1
16. I have a balanced view of taking risks in life.	5	4	3	2	1
17. I can make decisions and take action easily.	5	4	3	2	1
18. I take care of my health.	5	4	3	2	1
19. I often think about the deeper meaning of life.	5	4	3	2	1
20. I know I'm here for a reason and I know the direction I am going with my kids.	5	4	3	2	1

Now work out your score.

Between 20 and 40

Your confidence may be at a low point at the moment, but don't worry; it won't stay there for long. By regularly doing the exercises on the following pages you'll soon start to feel far more confident.

Between 40 and 60

You're nearly in the right zone, but you may be feeling a little uncertain or confused about your parenting. Give yourself time to relax and work on the areas that need your attention and you'll be amazed and really pleased by the progress you can make.

Between 60 and 80

Well done! You are pretty confident in most family situations and there are only a few areas that bring you down at the moment. Pat yourself on the back.

Between 80 and 100

That is brilliant! You are a really confident parent and you are clear on what is important to you, so celebrate your successes and keep going. Bringing up children is not an exact science, and you may find that your confidence can waver on a daily, weekly, or monthly basis, so read on to ensure you maintain your momentum.

Control Your Inner Bully and Nurture Your Inner Angel

Most of us are our own worst critics and we beat ourselves up with a negative inner voice inside our head. It's time to learn how to control and master those loud negative inner voices.

I want you to imagine that you have a control switch for the voices inside your head and therefore have complete control of the loudness and softness of them. Notice where the inner critic is located inside your head, and notice also where the inner angel or inner kindly voice is, as you are going to learn to turn up the inner angel – the kind, encouraging, nurturing voice – and to turn down, if not off, the harsh, critical, judgemental voice, to empower you with some simple, easy and effortless confidence.

Take your time, relax and start to slowly **turn down** the harsh, unkind, brutal voice of criticism until it is very hard to hear, and make the voice muffled and difficult to understand as if it is far away. Now turn **up** the gentle, nurturing, caring, compassionate voice that makes you feel good, more confident and self-assured. Bring that voice closer to your ears and really enjoy listening to the calm, reassuring, lovely words it has to say. Make it louder and clearer and in high definition so that you can really hear it, and enjoy receiving its encouraging, accepting message.

How does that feel?

You can turn down your inner bully any time you like. It's there to protect you from making a fool of yourself, stepping out of line or taking too much of a risk, but it can really hold you back and cripple your self-belief. So turn it off or turn it down and turn up your quieter inner angel. That nurturing, kind voice that whispers to you: 'You're really great at this,' 'You're really kind,' or 'You're really doing a great job!' This is the voice you should be listening to more often, so go on, be brave and turn this gentle, encouraging and positive voice up.

Easy Ways to Develop Your Confidence

So what do you think – is confidence won and lost, or is it something we are born with? We are all born with our own personality traits, but I think it is not so much who we are when we are born that counts, but whom we are encouraged and allowed to become. As a parent you have a big responsibility to support your child and develop this crucial belief in him. Are you ready for this amazing challenge?

> *'To respond to our children's needs, we must change ourselves. Only when we are willing to undergo the suffering of such changing can we become the kind of parents our children need us to be.'*
> ~ M. Scott Peck

Raising confident children begins with your own confidence. As your confidence grows, you will notice a real difference in yourself. The great benefit is that people around you will begin to see you in a different light and will react and treat you in new and positive ways, too. But most of all your kids will respond to you differently and in more positive ways as you exude this new confident, energetic and assertive attitude.

You are the most important role model in your child's life so it's really important that you genuinely feel positive, relaxed and confident every single day. Being happy, feeling relaxed and feeling positive is something that we all need each day if we are to withstand the ups and downs of family life. If you get used to putting yourself in a positive state each morning you'll notice an amazing change in your family life that will really improve your confidence as a parent, and will bring long lasting-benefits to your whole family.

The key thing to remember is: what you practise, you become. By working on your confidence you become more confident, and your parenting becomes easier and more rewarding.

I've done a great deal of research into what makes people happy, confident and well balanced and three key things seem to make a big difference: physical exercise, laughter and thinking positively.

Physical exercise is a natural way to use up the adrenaline released into your body due to stress and it also releases natural hormones called endorphins that make you feel good. So start your day by doing something physical, like stretching or running up and down the stairs a few times, or even going for a 20-minute walk.

The second thing to make you more confident is laughter. Laughter has been clinically proven to lift your spirits as it improves your mood and sense of wellbeing. It also releases endorphins, which makes you feel good; even just smiling releases something called serotonin, which is a natural way to relieve stress and get rid of negativity.

The third thing is thinking positively. Positive thinking and positive thoughts are absolutely crucial for becoming a confident parent, so start to focus on all the wonderful things in your life: the smiling faces of your kids, the lovely weather outside or your day ahead, and start to notice all the good things around you in great detail. By adopting 'the Attitude of Gratitude' you start to notice what's going well in your life and this can really lift your mood and you will seem to notice even more positive things – it's like an upbeat, self-fulfilling, positive prophecy. Even this simple idea of 'the Attitude of Gratitude' is one small step to becoming a more confident, positive and well-balanced parent.

Think about how you could do these simple, effective exercises on a regular basis so that you'll enjoy developing a new habit, which will make you feel happier, more confident and more motivated in your parenting.

Eliminate the 'Blame Game' Mentality

All family relationships are dynamic and they change over time. Part of being confident is to be able to handle change easily but one thing that can hold you back is the 'Blame Game'.

The Blame Game is not very helpful as it limits your choices and your results. If you constantly blame your partner, your kids, your own mum or dad, or your relatives, and find fault all the time in others, you aren't taking any responsibility for the results you get – and successful, positive and confident parents don't do that. They don't blame others or make excuses; they take it upon themselves to make a difference with their kids, and they don't expect others to shoulder the blame or bail them out.

Once you accept responsibility for yourself, your circumstances, your actions, thoughts and words, you are instantly empowered to make new and different choices and actually create a life of your own choosing rather than just accepting things as they are.

Try this little exercise to become aware of your attitude to your children, to circumstances and to situations that you find yourself in, as well as your attitude to taking responsibility for your own behaviour.

The camcorder, the police siren and the voice of choice

Imagine you have a camcorder sitting on your shoulder all day, which notices everything you do and everything you say. It notices the words you use with your kids, how you act with them, your tone of voice, body language and general mood throughout your whole day.

When you notice yourself making excuses or blaming someone else, hear the loud sound of a police siren ringing in your ears alerting you to danger, reminding you that you are forgetting to **choose** your behaviour, your mindset or your attitude and reminding you to take back control of your situation. Let the alarm bells remind you to say to yourself, 'So now what am I **choosing** to do about this situation?' By **choosing** how you react, you are taking back control and deliberately changing your perception. You are transforming your parenting relationships by choosing to feel more empowered by opening up to different possibilities. This will really improve your confidence and sense of being in control of your life simply by becoming more aware of the choices that you have available. You can **choose** how you want to react to your kids and you can **choose** the way you want to behave, act or speak – and the way you behave dictates the results you get.

Spring-cleaning your negative energy in this way and being aware of your old patterns of behaviour frees you up to have more positive energy and more fun; it also helps you to relax. We live in a hectic world full of school runs, football training, cooking meals and organising homework, but to feel confident and to function at your very best you need to feel balanced; and learning to control your thoughts, feelings and actions is very liberating and empowering.

Pressure Points and Toxic Moments

Think about the times and places where you feel constantly stressed. Is it early morning before the school run – what I call the 'Cornflake Conflict Time' – where you are constantly rushing around looking for school ties and bits of sports kit or frantically trying to make packed lunches? Or is it the running-on-empty time just before tea, when your kids are hungry, you're tired and the meal needs making?

Think of your pressure points and get them out in the open, because these toxic times are gradually sapping your confidence and you need to notice what's happening so that you can change things.

What's your number-one confidence and energy zapper, the thing that really drains you the most? What's the effect it's having on you and the family? If you could change this, what would be the biggest benefit to you? For example, if you got up 15 minutes earlier than the kids and then got them up, what benefits would you reap immediately? Or if you gave them a banana on the way home from school to take the edge off their hunger, made a cup of tea for yourself and had a 10-minute sit down before you started the dinner and the homework, what difference would that make?

Start thinking of new ways to do things that are practical. What's going to be your first step towards taking control of your energy- and confidence-zappers?

Another common confidence-drainer is taking on more and more and trying to do everything for everybody. Do you chase around your house helping to sort out everyone else? It's very easy to get caught in this trap but over time it drains all your energy and losing energy often means losing confidence, because your needs are not being met. Ask yourself: Do I have time for my hobbies, my friends and my other relationships? Do I take time out to rest, relax or exercise?

If the answer is no, perhaps you are supporting others in your family too much. Confident parents are generous to others, but they also make time for themselves. They value themselves, which builds up their confidence. Running around after everyone else can build up resentment and anger, which, left unresolved, can poison your relationships with your kids.

- What could you change this week to make more time for yourself?
- What would you like to do this week for yourself? Go to the cinema, read a magazine or meet a friend for a drink?

How to Stay Positive

It's not about who you are today as a parent that matters...it's all about who you are BECOMING!

I don't know about you, but I've made some BIG mistakes in my life at times, and I sometimes get stuck in the negative spiral of beating myself up, with my bullying, critical inner voice going on and on and on and on... Well, one day, after a particularly frustrating morning, I was having a little 'me' time, when I suddenly thought, 'What if I just saw myself as a "work in progress" and said to myself that I am "failing forward", always learning from my mistakes and always moving towards getting it right next time?' I suddenly felt loads better. I forgave myself for only being human, smiled inside and let the mistake go.

The Young Scientist's Inspiring Life Lesson

One of my favourite parenting stories is about a famous research scientist who made several important medical breakthroughs. The scientist was asked by a journalist why he was so successful and he told the story of a very early lesson he learnt from his mother when he dropped a carton of milk in the kitchen.

Instead of shouting at him, she said, 'What a wonderful mess you've made – what a huge great big puddle! I bet you'd love to play in that great big white milky puddle. Go on then – have some fun before we clean it all up!' After about 10 minutes his mum came back and continued, 'Well, you've had your fun so it's time to clear it all up. So, how would you like to do it – with a towel, a mop or a sponge?' They both spent some time on the clean-up operation and then his mum did a remarkable thing that in my opinion changed the little boy's destiny. She said, 'Let's go out in the garden and fill up the carton a few times so you can practise carrying it properly.'

The scientist remarked to the journalist that he knew right then and there that it was okay to make mistakes and he didn't have to be afraid of failing. He learnt that his mistakes were just opportunities for learning something new. I think this is an amazing story of a remarkable mother – transforming her perception of an accident and a mistake into a lifelong lesson.

Successful parents realise that making mistakes and getting things wrong is a really natural and important part of learning to be a great parent. They know that minor failures and setbacks are just the way we all learn – by trial and error. I call it 'failing forward' because being willing to learn from your mistakes and blips helps you to get brilliant feedback to correct and fine-tune your parenting, so you constantly keep moving forward.

Every experience will teach you something if you are open-minded and willing to let it. One of the secrets to successful parenting is to keep a positive focus no matter what's going on around you. Stay focused on your past successes rather than on your past mistakes or failures. Remember to keep your eye firmly on the prize, which is to bring up happy, confident well-balanced kids – today's children but tomorrow's future.

Don't beat yourself up

There's no such thing as a perfect parent, so why not just be the best you can be and relax? Don't be afraid to fail. Don't waste energy trying to cover up your failures or your mistakes. Learn from them and go on to the next challenge. Every experience will teach you something new. It's okay to fail. If you're not failing, you're not growing.

It's time to:

- Stop waiting for perfection
- Stop waiting for permission
- Stop waiting for reassurance
- Stop waiting for someone else to change
- Stop waiting for your kids to mature
- Stop waiting for someone else to give you all the answers
- Stop waiting for someone else to give you a clear set of instructions

'You can never learn less, you can only learn more. The reason I know so much is because I have made so many mistakes.'
~ Buckminster Fuller, Mathematician and Philosopher who never graduated from university but received 46 honorary doctorates.

Keep a 'Positive Parent Journal'

As parents, we are very hard on ourselves and tend to focus on what we don't do or manage to achieve throughout a typical day. A Positive Parent Journal is the first step to changing this negative attitude and I believe it is a simple but very important key to your success. As I have often mentioned before, being a parent is one of the most rewarding and enjoyable jobs you'll ever do in your life but it is also one of the most challenging, frustrating and exhausting.

By keeping your own journal or using the Positive Parent Journal that's available on my website (www.sueatkinsparentingcoach. com), you can keep a simple record of all the things you get right and learn to focus on the positive aspects of your parenting and your proudest achievements, no matter how small. I suggest that you record ALL the little things that went well, from smiling instead of frowning to speaking calmly in a difficult situation, and write them all down as this will keep you motivated, positive and upbeat. Keep focused on the long-term relationships you want to build with your children, as this keeps you out of the untidy-bedroom or undone-homework scenarios that most parents get stuck in. It stops you sweating the small stuff and gives you a wider and bigger perspective.

I suggest that you write in your journal last thing at night, as during the night your unconscious will replay and process what's gone on throughout your day and it remembers six times more strongly the last things you've seen, heard or read before you fall asleep – so why not make your last thoughts positive and uplifting? It's also why reading bedtime stories to your children is so impor-tant to them. It helps them feel safe and relaxed. This is a really wonderful way for you to fall asleep, and you will wake up the next morning feeling far more confident, hopeful and raring to go. After just a short time you will have developed a new and positive confident habit, which is the key to your success.

At the end of the week, look at your Positive Parent Journal and rate your achievements in order, from 1–7, with 1 being your greatest moment. Now read your chosen moments, and really enjoy, re-live and celebrate the warm feelings of success, achieve-ment and enjoyment. This is a very important aspect to your parenting confidence as it builds up your self-belief, and celebrat-ing is a brilliant and easy way to build success into your parenting.

The secret to always staying positive

I've read it many times and I've said it many times and I really think it's true – 'you get what you focus on'.

Positive parents tend to focus on what's going well, not on what could go wrong. They stay hopeful and therefore more positive things seem to happen to them. Positive parents, when faced with a challenge, difficulty or change, know that it is only a temporary setback and they focus on the future. Negative parents get stuck focusing on the problem and find it hard to see beyond it. Hopeful parents always see the glass as half full, not half empty!

Remember: staying hopeful and positive gets easier with practice as it becomes a mindset and a natural behaviour over time. Here are some more techniques to help you get into and stay in a positive frame of mind.

Positive body language

One simple strategy I use with parents is to get them to start to become aware of their body and how they use it to convey hidden messages. Just for this week, notice the way you walk, the way you talk and the way you use your body language when you are at home, in the office or out and about at the weekend. And practise using positive body language, as it is a really powerful tool to communicate your attitude to your kids.

To get yourself into a good positive state, first try smiling (even if you don't feel like it) as it releases natural endorphins which make you feel good immediately – it really works – go on, just try it! Tony Robbins – the famous peak performance coach – calls it changing your physiology and he swears by it. Start smiling or laughing, then try to feel negative or unconfident at the same time – it's impossible.

Positive words

Here is another way to help you get into a positive state: use only positive language and when you hear yourself slipping into negative words – just STOP!

Initially you will find it quite challenging to only use positive words, but over time you will get better and better at it. You'll find that it can really make a difference to your mood, attitude and confidence.

Seeing Things Differently

I've got a poster on the wall in my office that reframes negative statements into positive ones. It says:

'It's a problem .... Actually it's an opportunity'
'I'm never satisfied .... I want to learn and grow'
'Life's a struggle .... Life's an adventure'
'It's terrible .... It's a learning experience'

It really helps me to remember that life is all about your perception of things!

Remember that we all make mistakes and it's okay to make them – but it's churlish to keep making the same ones over and over again, so LEARN from them and let them go.

'Don't drive forward with your eyes firmly fixed on the rear-view mirror!'
~ Tony Robbins

Find Your Positive State at Any Time – The One Point

The One Point Exercise is a wonderful way to ground yourself and to feel centred, calm and back in control of your emotions regardless of what's going on around you. It's a simple way to change your attitude, mood or 'state' of mind – as I believe having a positive, upbeat, confident mindset is crucial to your parenting success as an effective and relaxed parent. This exercise empowers you to feel totally in control of any challenging situation in which you find yourself.

The key thing to remember again is that what you practise, you become, so relax, be curious and enjoy boosting your feeling of being in control of your emotions so that your life gets easier and more rewarding.

1. Relax and imagine yourself centred and grounded like an oak tree, with strong roots that go deep down into the earth. Now move your attention to a place just below your belly button, which is called your **'One Point'**. It's a place where your body is perfectly balanced and can't be swayed, knocked over or upset. It's a place of true control where you feel relaxed, balanced and unshakeable. Imagine yourself feeling wonderfully centred where nothing can upset or anger you, where you feel completely in control of everything around you.

2. Breathe deeply and slowly from this place of confidence and imagine breathing in a colour that represents confidence to you...

3. Let this colour spin down your body from the tip of your head to the bottom of your toes, fully enveloping you as it gives you this lovely feeling of inner and outer confidence. As you breathe out, exhale fear, anxiety, worry and guilt and watch it come out of your body easily.

4. From this place of confidence…relax.

5. Now imagine a situation that does upset, anger or frustrate you with your children and put your attention into your One Point, with all these grounded, centred and balanced feelings of control. And see what you would see, hear what you would hear and feel wonderfully centred and grounded.

6. Feel in control and confident and squeeze your right hand into a fist to remind you of these confident feelings. This is called an anchor and it will help you to feel relaxed and confident any time you squeeze your right hand into a fist.

7. Now come back into yourself and take all the positive and confident feelings back with you. Remember to use your One Point any time you feel flustered, angry or out of control. You now have a powerful tool that will get you back into the driving seat of your parenting every time you use it.

Focus on a positive outcome

If you remain calm and in control and remember to use your One Point, you can step back from an incident and quickly come up with lots of different ways to sort out the situation that suit everyone. It takes practice, and lots of it, but when you start to see the amazing shift in your family relationships it will totally transform your life.

Expect a positive and co-operative way of thinking with your family and over time you will achieve it easily and effortlessly… honestly!

Top 10 Points to Ponder as a Positive Parent

1. Children follow *you* first and what you say second – as a parent, who you are and how you act make a difference. The most important message you can share with your children is yourself.

2. Unconditional love, respect, trust and laughter are the key energies that connect you as a family – the glue that bonds you together, building the 'WE' mentality of a happy family able to withstand life's ups and downs.

3. Parenting is not just about what you do, but what you inspire, encourage and empower your children to do.

4. A parent brings out the best within their children by sharing the best within themselves.

5. Abraham Lincoln said, 'Most anyone can withstand adversity, but to test a man's character give him power.' The more power and influence you have as a parent the more it is your responsibility to serve, develop, nurture, empower and cherish your child's self-esteem and self-confidence – the true gift and legacy of parenting.

6. 'Rules without relationship leads to rebellion.' (Andy Stanley). This applies as much today to parents, as it ever did – particularly to parents of teenagers. Family life is all about relationships.

7. Be a positive, relaxed and confident parent – guard against pessimism and negativity as it disempowers, drains and holds children back from fulfilling and achieving their true unlimited potential.

8. Great parents know that they don't have all the answers – but they are confident enough to be open to new ideas and different ways of doing things.

9. Positive parents inspire and teach their children to focus on solutions, not mistakes. They ask: 'What did you learn?', not 'Who can you blame?'

10. Great parents know that success is a process not a destination.

A Final Word on Confidence

Confident parents seem to be surrounded by a clear sense of purpose as they have a really clear and definite idea of why they are taking a particular course of action. Positive and confident parents who set goals have more excitement and more positive energy because they are more motivated. They are more persistent, focusing on what they want. They find decision-making easy because they have a specific vision of the results they are trying to achieve and they keep the longer term, bigger picture in their mind. They also naturally pass this attitude on to their children. Confident and positive parents are usually great company because they're in the habit of seeing the bright side of life and expect good, positive experiences.

Children who are surrounded by positive, relaxed and confident parents develop positive thinking skills too and grow up expecting life to be generally good. Studies show that they also think and see the best in people and believe that most problems have a solution. Children from positive parents don't waste energy worrying about possible negative outcomes as they grow up focusing on the solutions.

It's simply that you are a role model. If you act and speak positively and confidently, your children will too.

3

Communicating Effectively With Your Kids

In this chapter we will be looking at one of the key habits of successful parents – developing effective communication skills and the ability to talk and listen easily to your children without shouting, nagging or pleading. Just as talking to your children is vital, no less important is the art of listening to them when they're talking to you. Communicating effectively with your children can make your role as a parent simpler, more enjoyable and ultimately a more fulfilling experience.

Everyone wants to feel understood, respected, heard and valued for who they are, and kids – whether they are a toddler, teen or tearaway – are, of course, no exception. That's why I believe it's really important to develop your skills in this area to build self-esteem, confidence and the lifetime bonds of love between you as a family. As parents, we all have a tendency to feel we 'know better' than our kids as we've 'been there, done that – and got the T-shirt'. We feel that we are older and wiser so we often don't really listen to what our kids are telling us – we presume, judge, make assumptions and often rush in to rescue them with our advice or suggestions.

We mean well – as we naturally have our kids' best interests at heart – but it doesn't really make for great relationships and lines of successful communication. There's a really lovely Native American Indian saying, which is: '*Listen or your tongue will make you deaf.*' This is so often the case, where we as parents talk so much that we forget to listen to our kids. I actually think nature is trying to tell us something, as we have two ears and one mouth for a reason – and I think that's a brilliant way to help us remember to listen first and talk later! Being a good, attentive and sophisticated listener is absolutely crucial to being a really successful, relaxed and great parent. This chapter looks at different types of communication and ways to improve your current approach to listening and talking to your kids, to make all your lives easier, more rewarding and more fun.

It's quite simple really, like most great truths in life: kids don't care how much you know, until they know just how much you care, so learning to listen attentively and empathetically is a really great place to start.

The Different Types of Listening

We're all guilty of it…hearing but not really listening to what our kids, mother-in-law or partner is actually saying to us, and there are loads of reasons why this happens – you may be juggling three things at once, like cooking the dinner, helping with homework and unloading the dishwasher, or you are just preoccupied with your own worries or to-do list. But actively and attentively listening are really important skills to develop as a parent as they can transform your relationships with your kids.

Our thinking speed is much faster than our talking speed and this is particularly true of children – especially the younger they are. This means that at times our brain is working way ahead of the person we are listening to – you may be preparing your reply long before the other person has even finished speaking. But this causes a lot of misunderstandings, arguments and incorrect actions and frustrations in families.

It's useful to know that there are three types of listening modes.

1. **Competitive or Combative Listening**, where the person who is talking is far more interested in promoting their point of view than listening, thinking and really considering the other person's point of view.

   You know how it feels when you're actually just waiting for a break in the flow of the other person's conversation so that you can get your penny's worth across. This is often when parents are really not absorbing their child's message and are just waiting to jump in and attack their child's point of view – and are always planning what they want to say next. They are actually just 'pretending' to listen to their kids. I see this a lot when I'm working with the parents of teenagers! This style of listening often results in arguments, frustrations and tears, with lots of misunderstandings and anger all round. But with some practice you can turn things around – easily and quickly.

2. **Passive or Attentive Listening**. This type of listening is where parents are genuinely interested in what's being chatted about but they don't really engage or connect with the conversation and stay rather aloof and outside the real energy of the conversation – this quietness can be interpreted by your children as being rather uninterested, which can also lead to misunderstandings amongst families.

3. **Active and Reflective Listening**. This type of listening is the one that I want to help you develop as it is the most successful form of communication for getting along well with

your children. Active and reflective listening happens when you are genuinely interested in your child's point of view or message. You sincerely want to know what your child is thinking, feeling and trying to say. Parents who listen actively join in and show they are interested by making little comments, nodding their head and listening carefully to show empathy before reacting. This listener is really effective as they also take the time to make sure they've understood what's been said to them.

This sort of listening is wonderful for making your kids feel heard and understood. Which takes me back to my key point: that it's a basic need of every child to feel heard, because when children feel heard they feel understood and can relax, and frustration, 'bad' behaviour and anger subsequently melt away.

Listening gremlins

But there are also five gremlins that prevent you from listening well:

1. Being preoccupied with your own worries, commitments or concerns so that you are 'miles away', worrying about deadlines, the dry-cleaning, school pick-ups or general family life-juggling.

2. Pretending to listen, where you say 'uh huh' or 'oh dear – that's terrible' or 'that sounds great' when you've not really taken on board what's been said to you properly as you were only half listening. It can all sound a bit patronising if you're not careful.

I remember doing that with my own mum when she had retired, when she wanted to tell me her stories about working in her charity shop, and I would pick up the paper and say 'hummm' and 'aaaah' from time to time – I feel awful now when I look back, as she must have felt ignored and unimportant. Your kids will pick up on those times when you're too busy peeling the potatoes or unloading the dishwasher and are not really listening to them – over time they will stop talking to you.

3. 'Selective listening', where you only pay attention to the parts of the conversation that interest you and respond only to those bits – which actually hijacks the other person's conversation or takes the conversation on to your agenda, making the other person feel frustrated and sometimes annoyed.

4. 'Words only' listening, where you hear only the actual words being said but don't pick up on the hidden agenda underneath the meaning – like when my husband says to me, 'Are you okay?' and I reply, 'Yeah…fine,' when I really mean, 'No I'm hacked off that you left your shoes out in front of the bed again and I tripped over them.'

5. The self-centred type of listening when you only see things from your point of view – when you are not really seeing the situation or the story from the view of your child. You actually want your child to see the world from your shoes and to stand in them.

This sort of listening can turn into one-upmanship where there has to be a winner and a loser – as if the communication is a competition. The 'You think you've had a bad day…that's nothing…let me tell you about my day…' scenario.

When you listen to your kids from the 'me' type of mode you can fall into the nasty trap of judging, advising or probing them too much. For example, when you only listen from your point of view, you make presumptions and judgements based on your experiences and expectations of the world – not your kids' – and you can forget that everyone is different and experiences the world in their own way. So when you are judging, you have already closed down and are not really listening or being curious or open-minded about your child.

Hear What Your Children Are Saying to You

Your kids don't want to be judged – they want to be heard. Try to avoid falling into the trap of giving advice based on your experience – the 'when I was your age' sort of scenario – which may not actually be relevant to your child's situation or experience. Of course, we all do it, but try to become aware of it so that you can change it.

For example, when my daughter Molly came home from school and started chatting about being made to play Goal Keeper in her netball team instead of her favourite position of Goal Defence, my son (who is two years older) got into his 'older brother, I know better than you' mode and said, 'Oh you need to be flexible in your attitude – I remember when I was playing in my football team and...' By then, my daughter had switched off and got huffy as she didn't want advice from her older brother, no matter how sensible it was. She just wanted to be listened to, given room to moan, to feel heard and understood.

My poor son learnt a valuable lesson about listening – particularly to women! – that I think will serve him in good stead later on in life. It showed him how to listen to someone when all they need is to be heard.

Asking Good Questions

For me, questions are the currency of good communication and are very powerful as they help avoid confusion and aid understanding. But as parents we often don't stand back and think about how we speak or listen to our children, or the sorts of questions we ask our kids.

The key to really effective communication is in asking the right questions and then sitting back to properly listen to the answers. In fact, as parents you have a huge impact on the development of your children's language skills and mental development by the way you ask them questions. You really help your kids to develop their thought processes and ability to communicate by making them think properly about an answer.

Research has shown that kids who are able to communicate effectively through being talked to openly are less frustrated at home – or at school – and are kinder to other people. They are able to talk on many levels with people of all ages and backgrounds and can read other children's body language more easily. They learn to discuss rationally rather than shout, and even have enough confidence to speak in public. All this comes from the types of questions you get used to asking them!

One thing parents often do that puts kids off communicating is to probe too deeply before the child is ready to open up. Kids don't like to be interrogated by lots of questions when they're not ready to talk. I often found that my son would open up to talk just as I was about to climb into my long-awaited bubble bath or my soft, warm bed after a tough day of teaching – but I was flexible enough to take the long-term view, which was that listening and chatting would build our relationship. If you listen to them when they are four, hopefully they will still be talking to you at fourteen!

Open-ended questions

There's a huge difference between 'talking at' and 'talking with' your child. Rather like 'laughing at' or 'laughing with' someone. As parents, you need to guard against the conversation that feels like a lecture, inquisition or nag, and asking open-ended questions will really change the feel of your conversation and move it away from the 'talking at' mode.

An open-ended question is one that needs a descriptive answer and is quite elaborate, whereas a closed question can be answered really quickly with a short 'Yes' or 'No' reply.

Here are some examples of open-ended questions:

- How...?
- What...?
- Where...?
- When...?
- Who...?
- How much...?

However, it's often a good idea to avoid the 'Why...?' question as it tends to make children feel defensive as if you are criticising them. Think of how you'd feel if someone said:

- 'So why did you spill the breakfast cereal all over the table?'
- 'Why didn't you ring me at 10 o'clock like you said you would?'

In your mind, go over some new types of questions. Imagine yourself becoming more aware of the types of questions you ask and paying attention to the new ways of speaking to your children, preparing yourself for longer answers and more interesting chats with your kids.

Imagine asking questions like:

- How was your lunch today?
- What did you get up to at playtime?
- What was the most exciting part of your day?
- Who made who laugh at school today?
- What was the best thing about your week?

Visualise the conversations going really well and becoming more involved – see what you'll be doing and what your kids will be doing, hear what you'll be saying and what your kids will be saying, and imagine all the great feelings of fun, laughter and the achievements of building a better relationship with your kids.

Just for this week, practise asking your children open-ended questions; notice how your conversations expand and become far more interesting and enjoy learning more about your children's lives, thoughts and experiences. This might feel a bit strange at first, as you are developing a new habit, but like everything in life, the more you do it the more it will become natural to you. At the beginning, put Post-it notes in your handbag or pocket or somewhere that will remind you of the types of new questions you want to start asking your children. Parents often find a dramatic improvement not only in the quality of their conversations, but in the length and enjoyment of their exchanges too and everyone seems to enjoy this new way of communicating together.

Consider Your Tone of Voice

When I was a child, I could tell if I was in trouble by the way my mum spoke to me. If she called me by my full name, 'Susan', I knew something was up. It wasn't just the words she used – her tone of voice usually had an edge to it.

Children are extremely sensitive to tone of voice, so this week, start to notice and make a mental note of when you use a sarcastic or angry tone with them, or an encouraging, gentle and sympathetic tone. Also notice what has happened just before it – are you reacting to your kids or were you in control first? Which tones of voice create harmony, and which don't?

If you become more aware of when you slip into your Cruella de Vil voice, you are more likely to press your pause button, step back and change your tone.

Don't match your child's tone

It's also worth remembering not to match the tone used by your child. When your children provoke you with their plaintive crying, tantrums or whining, it can be very hard to remain calm. If you let your temper get the better of you and can't help but match their tone, things may escalate until you have World War III on your hands!

How can you put a stop to it? If someone whines at you it's easy to answer in a whiny voice. Resist doing this and instead try to respond in a pleasant, no-nonsense manner. This is the key to changing any type of unacceptable tone – simply do not match it.

The trouble is that many of us don't realise when we are caught up in the tone game. It may well be the tone that we use with our children that gets them into trouble in the first place. If you've ever heard your child repeating your exact words back you or to someone else, you'll know how easily they absorb and mimic your tone of voice.

Pause here and ask yourself the questions below. Jot down the answers, as putting things in writing really clarifies your thoughts properly. Ask yourself:

- How could you change the atmosphere by using a different tone of voice? Imagine yourself handling the situation easily and effortlessly, using a new technique or a new tone of voice. Imagine what you see, what you hear and how you feel, and make the sounds and pictures brighter and louder. Enjoy the lovely feelings of success as you handle this usually challenging situation in a different and more effective way.

- What phrase or simple expression could you use that would make everyone feel more positive and might even make everyone laugh, which is a great tension breaker?

Try remembering to do some of these things:

- Be aware of what is an inappropriate way for your child to speak to you. If you hear them using this tone, resist responding in the same manner.

- Keep calm, press your 'pause' button and think about your response before you give it.

- Talk in a very sweet tone – it will help you to recognise how you should sound, and although it might feel silly, with practice you'll sound natural.

- When your child speaks to you in a normal, neutral voice, make sure you acknowledge this and praise them for it. Your child will realise that they don't have to whine or shout to be heard and their self-esteem will be boosted.

How Sympathetic Are You?

It distresses me to hear parents telling their children to 'shut up' or say things that humiliate or embarrass them in front of other people. I've heard loads of parents berate their kids, interrupt them, not pay real attention to them and speak to others in front of them as if they don't exist. I suppose they're demonstrating that they have the upper hand and are more powerful. Unfortunately, these actions do nothing to build a child's self-esteem, create family unity or enhance the communication between you.

How sympathetic are you when your child is trying to talk to you? More important than all the words you use is your attitude. If your attitude is not one of understanding, compassion or sympathy then whatever you say will be seen as insincere, false and uncaring in your child's eyes. It takes thought and effort to let your child know that you have a sense of what they must be going through and sometimes that really doesn't come naturally to us. It's so important to let your child have time to formulate their sentences and finish what they want to say, as children think slightly slower than adults and when you cut your child off or finish their sentence for them you are sending the message that you don't really care what they have to say and this can destroy loving communication.

Quick Tips to Improve Your Communication Skills

It is really, really important when you are communicating with children that you are extremely clear about what you want to happen, use short instructions and mean what you say, so that kids get the message quickly, effectively and sense your energy and attitude. So be clear, concise and mean business!

Parents often fall into the trap of communicating from different rooms so the noise level just goes up and up and it is impossible for your child to see your face, hear the urgency in your voice or actually know that you mean what you say. Most kids don't really appear to listen but they actually hear everything you say.

There are also other things to think about when you are communicating with your child. Let's look at some key ways of talking to your kids to see how you are doing at the moment. After you've read through the list below, pause and think about each one and how you use these skills yourself at the moment. Make some written notes to keep you on track if it helps.

Do you:

- Say what you mean and mean what you say?
- Talk positively to your kids or nag and moan?
- Communicate calmly in difficult or challenging situations?
- Have an awareness of how you listen?
- Talk 'at' not 'with' them?
- Ask open-ended questions?
- Create quality talk time and put aside special time each day to actively listen and chat with your kids?

How do you rate yourself on the above communication skills at the moment on a scale of 1–10 (10 being brilliant and 1 being lousy)? Once you have rated yourself for each skill, you will be able to answer the following:

- Which of these talking or listening communication skills would you say you are really good at?
- Which one is your least effective?
- What do you think is the reason for that?
- If you could develop and improve in just one area, which one would you choose?
- Relax and think about how improving in just that area would affect the quality of your communication and relationship with your child.

Make a commitment to yourself today to practise just one area at a time and record your results in your Positive Parent Journal or notebook over the next week to see how you get on – then choose another one to work on during the following week and enjoy the feelings of moving forward positively and noticing the improvements in your family relationships. Be patient: family relationships and new skills take time to mature – like fine wine!

I like this quote from Paul Tillich: '*The first duty of love is to listen.*' How would that affect the quality of your relationships with your family? Perhaps you'd like to use more positive language with your children, be more upbeat in your tone, calmer in challenging situations or really listen to your child's side of the story by stopping what you're doing. Or perhaps you'd like to listen with your eyes and really look into your child's eyes when they are talking to you, or talk with, not *at*, them. Maybe you'd like to ask more open-ended questions or even just make more time to talk and chat with them.

This is a wonderful opportunity to step away from the humdrum, mundane routines and look more objectively at your communication skills. Here are some practical tips to help you along the way, which I have found to be invaluable with my own kids.

1. The first thing to do is to stop what you are doing

Have you ever tried telling someone something really exciting or interesting to you, but they have kept on reading the paper or watching the telly? It is really awful trying to talk to someone who is only paying you lip service and pretending to listen to you. It's much easier to tell your worries or successes to someone who is really listening, and as a parent you can listen really easily just by stopping what you are doing for a few minutes to give your child your full attention. Often it's the sympathetic or happy silence that makes all the difference.

2. Listen with your eyes

Active listening means that you are intentionally focusing on who you are listening to, so that your toddler or teen feels valued and heard, and you understand what they are saying. As the listener, you should then be able to repeat back in your own words in your head what they have said to you. This does not mean you agree, but rather that you understand what they are saying. Look into your child's eyes to show them that you are really listening. This helps to make effective listening into a habit.

3. Listen with your heart

Turn to face your child so that your heart is facing your child's heart; this will help you to remember to concentrate and completely focus on what your child is saying when they speak to you. It also reminds you that you love them, even if you are busy. It's a simple tip but it means you are not judging, as you are just loving your child unconditionally by listening from your heart. Listen with your eyes and your heart and don't be in a hurry – stay focused and empathetic. Give your child the gift of self-esteem by turning towards them and looking at them properly when they speak to you.

Learn to Listen Actively

We've all met people who are excellent communicators, people who make you feel good after you have spent time with them.

They seem genuinely enthusiastic and interested in you. So how are they doing this?

They are 'actively' listening – a skill that all great communicators use naturally or learn to develop and they are establishing rapport with you first, by relaxing and matching your body language, speed of speaking, rhythm of breathing and way of speaking – they are really engaged in what you are saying and genuinely interested in what you are talking about.

In the workshops I run, I often spend a great deal of time helping parents to improve their rapport skills as this creates a great starting block on which to build. Observe, and listen to, the ways *your child* uses language so that you can copy it. Become aware of matching their speed of speech, their body language and breathing, and notice the types of language they use – the words they use – and use the same type of words back. For example, do they say things like: 'I **see** what you mean,' or, 'I don't think we're on the same **wavelength** Mum – you never listen to me,' or, 'I feel all wobbly inside'? We all use language in different ways and if you can use the same sort of language as your kids they will feel more rapport with you and that they are properly understood and heard. You will notice a vast improvement in your family relationships by simply mirroring your child's ways of communicating in this manner.

✓ Learn and develop the skill of **reflective listening**, which is like acting as a mirror for your kids to bounce off. Imagine you are a long, stylish full-length mirror – to reflect the beauty, enthusiasm and joy of your children when they are speaking to you and to reflect back the message that they are trying to convey to you with the underlying emotion. Remember that mirrors can't give advice or judge – they can only reflect!

Reflective listening is also known as mirroring when you repeat back what your child has said to you and how they feel about it, but this isn't mimicking or teasing. Mimicking like a mynah bird or parrot and just squawking back the exact words your child has said to you, or repeating back the same words sounding cold, aloof and indifferent to the meaning behind them, can be really annoying and patronising, whereas mirroring or paraphrasing sounds warm, caring and searching, giving clarity to your child's feelings and the sense that you want to understand what they are trying to say to you.

Use your common sense and don't go into reflective listening when your three-year-old son says, while you're out shopping, 'I need to go to the toilet,' and you reply, 'So what you're really saying is that you are anxious that we won't be able to find a toilet in time?' There's a time and a place for everything.

Consistency

The biggest single contributor to your child's disciplinary problems is inconsistent parenting.

You're probably thinking, 'Well being consistent is easy to say, but hard to do,' but the secret is to keep your expectations clear and always meet the same behaviour with the same reaction.

It doesn't matter whether you use stickers, the naughty step, time-out in their bedroom, loss of TV time or whatever your choice of discipline, but make sure you enforce your rules and expectations with total consistency. If you are having trouble disciplining your child, the first thing you should do is take a step back and ask yourself, 'Am I being consistent?'

There are many reasons why parents become inconsistent but one of the main ones I see is stress and tiredness. In today's hectic and frenetic world we all get tired and that's when we feel like giving in or can't quite find the energy to take on the battle or argument that's probably going to ensue – it's easy to get distracted or lose our focus. It's also likely to happen if you are going through a major change like going back to work, going through a divorce, moving house or bonding a new stepfamily together.

It's easier to be consistent if you have routines, because consistency in routines breeds consistency in your parenting. When life is unpredictable it's easy to get distracted.

A lot of parents whom I coach ask whether it's important to maintain a united front in their discipline and the simple answer is that it depends on your child's age. Younger children need a totally united front so they know where they are, as they see the world in black and white, whereas, with slightly older children and teenagers, it isn't absolutely necessary as older children can reason and see two sides to an argument. It's always a good idea to chat with your partner over important things and to make sure that you are in agreement. An important point here is to make sure that your children aren't playing you against each other!

Ask yourself these questions:

- How consistent are you in what you say to your children?
- Would you say your actions speak louder than your words?
- How easily do you forgive your children?
- Would you say you give a genuine apology when you are wrong?

If you're not so happy with what you've discovered when answering these questions just think about changing some aspect of what you're currently doing this week. Making a small change can often make a big difference. Consistency is really about building trust and is a vital part of your toolkit when it comes to discipline.

Helping Children
Handle Their Feelings

How kids feel affects how they behave – so when they feel happy and understood, they are more likely to behave well. By practising some of the techniques in this chapter you can help your kids feel understood and improve their behaviour and attitudes.

Take some time this week to observe just how you respond to your children – do you say things like:

- 'You can't be too hot...put your jumper back on...'
- 'Why didn't you have a good time – it was lovely.'
- 'What do you mean the film was boring...I thought it was really exciting...'
- 'Well the teacher was cross, so you must have done something wrong.'

As parents we have a natural habit of denying or disregarding our children's emotions, feelings and experiences. Perhaps your parents did this to you when you were growing up and you've fallen into the same pattern. It is quite a challenge for us to change our parenting habits. But denying how your child feels prevents good communication and makes your kids feel annoyed, confused and frustrated with you. When things upset us, we all need someone to listen. Just imagine how you'd feel if your emotions were brushed aside like this by your family or friends.

Practising empathy

To help your child deal with their feelings, a good strategy is to simply acknowledge those feelings. Make it clear you are listening to them by nodding or making encouraging noises. Don't start giving your child your own opinions on the situation. Your kids will feel supported, not judged, and it will strengthen communication between you as your child will feel that they have a listening ear and a sympathetic parent who gives them the time they need to express themselves.

Empathy is a key skill to learn if you are to become a better parent and often we are so busy that we haven't got the time or patience to really listen empathetically. Empathy is the ability to understand the feelings of another and to identify with them. Just by understanding how your child feels, you are on the road to practising this really important skill that will transform your family's way of communicating, making it more effective and successful.

Here are some ways to practise the skill of empathetic listening by reflecting on these simple everyday examples:

1. *'Susie made fun of me today at school and everybody laughed.'*
Find a word that describes what your child is feeling. Perhaps it's upset. Now think about a sentence that sounds natural and empathetic and shows that you understand what emotion your child must have been feeling.

'Ohh Sophie, that must have been really upsetting for you.'
Simply by acknowledging your child's emotion, you are reacting to them in an empathetic way and your child will feel understood, supported and listened to.

2. *'I wish that Will would stop talking all the time in class! I can't get my work done.'*
Again find a word that describes what your child is feeling. Perhaps it's irritation. Use it in a sentence that recognises the emotion your child is feeling.

'*Ohh, it sounds like Will is really irritating.*'

This may feel or sound rather obvious to you, but it shows your children that you can empathise with them and understand their emotion, and this part can actually take a bit of practice. Many parents get worried that by acknowledging their child's emotions they will somehow make things worse, but children really appreciate when you understand how they feel. They find it comforting.

Sometimes just having someone around that genuinely understands how much you really want something makes the reality of not having it easier to bear. One quick strategy is to turn their wants into a game – just be mindful that you don't appear to be teasing or 'laughing' at them.

Here's an example of how this strategy works.

'*I really want fish fingers!*'

'*Oh Carrie, what a shame we've eaten them all last week. I really wish I had some in the freezer right now for you!*'

'*I want them!*'

'*Yes I can tell just how much you want them. If only I had a super submarine that could whisk me into the ocean to catch some fish and bring me back in time for dinner super quickly! So what do you fancy instead?*'

'*I really wish you had a super submarine that could do that... Okay, can we have...potato waffles instead?*'

'*Great – no problem, I'll get moving on that then.*'

I've seen this work really well with my own children as well as other families – so here's a quick reminder that you could copy and put up somewhere where you can see it easily and be reminded often, to help this turn into a new habit.

Handling Your Child's Feelings Positively

All children need to have their feelings accepted, respected and understood, so remember to:

1. Listen quietly and attentively.
2. Acknowledge their feelings with one simple remark: 'Oh... Mmmm... I see...'
3. Give their feeling a name: 'That sounds *frustrating*!'
4. Make your child's wish come true – in a daydream: 'I wish I could make the rain disappear for you!'

Of course, while you accept all of your child's feelings, you must make it really clear that certain actions are always unacceptable and must be limited – like kicking, hitting or pushing. So be clear by saying something like, 'I can really tell how angry you are with your sister but you can only tell her in words. Don't hit her.'

Respecting that your child's emotions may be different from yours

Empathising with your children can take a great deal of effort but practising this way of communicating with them will give them massive comfort in knowing that their feelings are understood and that they are not being negated, dismissed, ridiculed, trivialised or undermined. Simply hold back from giving advice or dismissing their emotions if they are different from yours – no matter how tempting it is.

Here's a little experiment to try. For the next week, have conversations with your children where you just accept their feelings and acknowledge them. Don't sound patronising or condescending by repeating their words back too exactly, but practise accepting their emotions even if they are different to yours. Your children are going to find this 'new you' surprising and it may feel awkward at first for you – but stick with it and you will see ENORMOUS benefits to your family relationships, I guarantee.

How to gain co-operation from your children

Of course children need to behave in certain ways that are acceptable to you as a family and also in society as a whole, but does it all sometimes feel like one big NAGGING session? It can feel like an uphill struggle some days with no end in sight, and it's also one of the built-in frustrations of parenthood that no one bothered to tell you!

Write down all the things you insist that your children do during a typical day – the things you nag about – to get them out of your system. Consider how much energy, time and effort you are expending on getting your kids to do as you want. For example, tidying up after they have finished with something, putting the tops back on the bottles, eating plenty of fruit, etc.

Next try the following different methods when you come across a naggable offence:

- **Describe the problem.**
  For example, if there were dirty clothes all over my son's room, I would say: '*I see a load of dirty clothes over the floor in your bedroom. I don't like having to walk around picking them all up.*'

- **Give instructions.**
  Making a statement or giving your child further information is a lot easier for them to hear than an accusation. So try saying

something like, '*When you've worn something, it goes in the laundry basket.*'

● **Use a simple phrase.**
You can reinforce your point with a simple phrase, such as: '*The laundry basket!*'

● **Talk about YOUR feelings.**
Be honest with your kids about how these issues make you feel, so that they can understand why you're upset without feeling hurt or accused. This maintains respect all round. I might say, '*It annoys me when the clothes aren't in the basket. It takes up lots of my time when I have to go hunting for them and it hurts my back when I have to bend down picking them all off the floor.*'

● **Say it with a note.**
Or you could try writing an amusing note. I know it seems quite wacky, but there's nothing quite like the power of the written word, particularly if it's light-hearted in tone.

> *Dear Molly*
> *We would really like to have a go in the washing machine as we've heard from the other clothes that it's like a roller-coaster ride. Would you be able to give us a real treat and pop us in the laundry basket so we can try it out for ourselves?*
> *Thanks*
> *Your Clothes*

These methods help get your kids' co-operation while keeping the atmosphere light and friendly. Be genuine and patient and don't expect it to work perfectly straight away – you may have to practise as a family for quite a while. Keep a note of all your successes and remind yourself of them whenever you need some encouragement to keep going.

Talk Time

I always took my son to his football training on a Thursday evening and often I used to find the 30-minute drive in the rush hour a bit of a chore – but gradually I changed my perspective of the time together and saw it as a great opportunity for us to chat about his day or his week, his thoughts, or life in general, and it turned into a chance for us to laugh about nothing in particular or just sit in a natural silence but feel together. It was also a regular slot when we both knew we would be able to chat through anything that was worrying him. This became our 'talk and listen time' and I really looked forward to it.

Think about a time that could be regular and natural for you to ring-fence as a time to chat to one or all of your kids – somewhere you are not going to be stressed or hassled and a time that can fit in naturally and regularly to your busy lives.

Children never 'outgrow' the need for quality talk time with you – I still miss the long chats I used to have with my dad when he was alive, about curtains, carpets, kids, gardening, life in general or nothing much in particular, because sharing thoughts and feelings and being together is what family life is all about.

Spending quality talk time with your children sends out the message that they are important, valued and loved. It will also teach them how to communicate and become eloquent and help them develop proper relationships with others naturally and easily. For many families, eating together provides the natural place for this to happen – if you are a busy family then this might be a good time for you all to sit down and just chat together.

Make a note of your own 'special talk time', keep to it regularly and watch your relationships flourish as a result.

Family meetings

As well as quality one-on-one time with your children, family chats or 'family meetings' are also a great way to sort out the usual ups and downs of family life as they help you all go in the same direction together and get things out in the open. Getting your kids involved is a nice opportunity to make them feel part of the decision-making process at home, as creating solutions to family niggles provides a real incentive for everyone to co-operate.

Having a regular family meeting is also a great time to sort out your plans and schedules for the coming week so that no one feels left out or doesn't know what everyone else is up to, as well as being a good place to discuss your family rules and the consequences for breaking them. Why not use this opportunity to look at how the jobs and chores are getting done in your house and use it as a way to sort out who does what and when?

But the real benefits to having a family talk-time routine is that you all come together to chat, relax and work as a 'family team', communicating, laughing, negotiating, sharing, spending quality time together and learning to pass on your rules, values and family ethos to your kids in a natural and informal setting. It irons out niggles, worries and problems and helps you to stay connected to your children and actively involved in their lives. So when your children hit the teenage zone and become more uncommunicative, you have a simple mechanism in place to help keep the lines of communication open. Finally, it's a good idea to relax and have fun together, so set aside a short period of time when the meeting is over to play a game together as a family so that your children have quality time with you and look forward to the meetings.

If you like the sound of having regular family chats with a purpose and that let you involve your kids, sort out the usual ups and downs of family life and help you all grow together, here are some ways to organise yourselves.

Tips for family talk time
- Develop a set of 'Family Meeting Rules' at your first meeting and be sure to write them down so everyone is clear about what to expect.
- Have the family meeting at the same time and place each week or month as it builds routine and expectations.
- Make sure that ALL your family members are present and have a chance to be heard.
- It's often a good idea to put all decisions from the meeting in writing and have everyone sign the sheet when the meeting ends to show their commitment to what's been talked about and agreed – get one of the kids to design it on the computer!
- Keep the meeting positive and have rules against disrespectful behaviours such as interrupting, insulting, or yelling or laughing at other people's suggestions.
- Avoid distractions – so turn off the TV and radio, take the phone off the hook, etc., so that you can relax and enjoy chatting together.

Remember that the chat or family meeting has a purpose, which is to spend constructive, quality time discussing the concerns and issues that need to be addressed. So think of it like a business meeting but with a more relaxed atmosphere – and plan an agenda.

Have a simple agenda
Having an agenda sounds a very formal idea but really it's just making sure that you have a structure and plan to your conversation,

otherwise you can get lost among the usual interruptions. Keeping to a simple plan helps you to discuss progress, problems and changes over the week. It helps you to decide on solutions, so it keeps you focused and always moving forward. Encourage everyone to give positive feedback to each other and have the intention of an upbeat, positive meeting, not a whining, negative, critical moan.

Here are some suggestions for agenda topics that are really fascinating to explore with your whole family, either once a week, once a month or now and again – whatever suits the rhythm and style of your family.

- **Self-esteem:** What is it about yourself that you are most proud of?
- **Taking initiative:** Name three things that you have done lately to demonstrate initiative.
- **Being helpful:** Who was the last person that helped you? How did they help and how did you feel?
- **Being responsible:** What can you do this week to show that you are being responsible?
- **Choices and consequences:** Chat about the best choice that you have ever made. What was the worst choice?
- **Safety:** What safety rules are in place in your home? How do these rules keep your kids safe?
- **Fairness:** Give some examples of things in your life that you think are unfair.
- **Managing anger and frustration:** What do you do when you feel annoyed or angry with someone in the family – what could you do instead?
- **Honesty:** Why is it important to be honest?
- **Friendship:** What do you look for in a friend?
- **Relaxation:** Do you ever have times when you find it difficult to relax? When? Why?

- **Plan a family outing:** Plan an outing for the whole family to participate in (within the next month).
- **Attitude:** What do you think causes people to have a negative attitude?

Now that you've got the idea, create your own topics for 'Family Talk Time'. These regular meetings give you an opportunity to come together – to learn, chat and watch your relationships grow, develop and flourish. I also recommend the very wonderful Fink Cards by Lisa Warner as a great way to get your family talking, having fun and communicating easily.

How Are You Communicating at the Moment?

It's time to assess your current ways of communicating with your kids so that you can see what you'd like to fine-tune or improve. Take a few moments now to visualise what happens when your kids start to talk or chat to you. What are you doing? What are you feeling? How are you standing? What tone of voice do you use? What's your body language unconsciously saying to them?

Now float into the shoes and socks of your kids – imagine you are your son or daughter. See through their eyes, hear through their ears, feel how they feel.

Now bring back all the learning and new insights from that experience into the present moment. What did you discover? If you could improve on those scenarios what would you like to change this week?

The Key Principles for Good Communication

- Communication should be open-ended, not closed. For example: 'Tell me about how the school trip went,' rather than, 'Did you enjoy the school trip?'
- It must be a two-way thing. It's not just about you telling your child something or giving advice, but rather listening to their viewpoint and accepting their emotions.
- Reflective listening is the most effective way of communicating with your kids, where you recognise, respect and acknowledge your child's views and worries.

  Look for the emotional meaning that often lies behind the words, identify the feeling and feed it back. Say something like: 'So you must have felt really angry when that happened.' You can also reflect back the content of what your child is saying to clarify points and make sure you've understood: 'You mean your best friend Christy will be leaving at the end of term?'

Remember that talking is only part of the communication process. Listening is an important skill too. Stop what you're doing and give your full attention to your child.

- Make eye contact.
- Don't interrupt too quickly.
- Give prompts – nodding, smiling, and saying 'Mmmm' to show interest.
- Make it clear that you're always willing to listen sympathetically, whether it's about a falling-out with a best friend, a failure to get into a football or netball team, or disappointing marks in an exam. Make sure you emphasise that making mistakes is the way to learn how to get things right, not just about failure.

Developing the ability to both talk and listen so that your kids will open up to you is a life-long challenge but, once you have become aware of its importance and value in your family relationships, I hope it is one that you will feel is worth the effort.

I really think that the topics covered in this chapter could be the most important in the whole book, because if you can become an effective communicator and, equally importantly, encourage your children to communicate confidently, then not only are you heading for a harmonious home life but you are also preparing your children to make the most of all the opportunities in life that will come their way.

So be patient with yourself and your kids, be tolerant and have the highest of intentions for yourself and your family. Remember that a smile is a curve that puts a lot of things straight, so laugh and grow together and learn to build bridges, not walls, of communication and your family life will become more rewarding, enjoyable and fulfilling.

4

Discipline – The Secret to Well-behaved Kids

Do you find disciplining your children difficult? The funny thing about discipline is that you only really notice it when it's not there. When I was a deputy head I saw loads of perfectly well-behaved kids, who I'd been teaching all day, run out into the playground to meet their parents and turn into children from hell – horrible, out-of-control monsters, whining, moaning, demanding and running wild, while their confused and baffled parents looked on helplessly wondering what to do or say to rein them in.

We all know parents, friends and even family who are out of control: the kids you dread to see at the front door because they whine all afternoon, beat up your cat or your kids and demand 'juice' all the time. Or the parents who let their kids stay up all night on the computer or MSN chatting and talking, allow them to come home at all hours and give them alcopops or beer when they are only 14.

Getting co-operation from kids has never been easy. But how come some parents have got it sorted? What's their magic formula? What are these parents doing 'right'? Well, parents who are successfully disciplining their kids do it for one simple reason: **It makes life with children easier.**

Disciplining your kids fairly, and firmly, makes your life easier and more rewarding. It makes your life and theirs run more smoothly in the long run and taking the long-term view is crucial to successful parenting, whether it is in deciding the destination of your parenting in the first place or setting boundaries and rules. Giving kids discipline is vital and, in my opinion, as important as unconditional love. Giving in to kids doesn't make your life easier – it sends out the message that you don't care enough about your own principles or about your children to set them boundaries based on love. By not setting clear, concise boundaries, everyone's life is more chaotic, stressful and insecure as no one knows exactly where they are.

This chapter gives you some simple tools to make disciplining your kids easier, using methods that work quickly and effectively. It provides straightforward solutions so that you can all get on with the business of living your lives in more harmony, able to have more fun, and to relax and enjoy your family life.

Give Your Children the Gift of Self-discipline

Kids who are taught through loving, fair discipline are happier, feel more secure, do better at school, don't go off the rails so easily with drugs or drink, and negotiate and function in the world far more easily. Without rules and parental guidelines kids don't develop their own inner controls and they may carry on 'throwing their toys out of the pram' whether they are six or even sixteen! So by teaching discipline you are teaching autonomy and preparing your kids to live in the real world with rules, regulations and limitations, and to contribute to society, not abuse it. If you don't set firm, fair and consistent boundaries for your kids, their school, the police, social services or the courts will instead.

Your kids 'catch' behaviour habits from you. This includes shouting, swearing, arguing or getting angry in order to win. So lesson number one is that it's important to set boundaries and to defend them.

Children like to know where they stand. So routines, boundaries and structures give children security and help them understand what acceptable behaviour is. By following, accepting and understanding your limits, your kids learn autonomy and self-control – which is a crucial life skill. From the age of two, start talking to them about your rules and limits and explaining why you have these and what you expect from them. This gives your kids an understanding about where you're coming from, but do make your explanations appropriate and relevant to their age.

For example, your two-year-old may want ice cream for breakfast, because they have no understanding of what a healthy diet is, so explain to your young child why they need to eat their cereal or fruit for breakfast and have ice cream as a treat. Use this as an opportunity to talk and teach your child about what a healthy little one needs to grow up big and strong.

Talk to your six-year-old about why they have to go to bed at a regular time – explain that sleep is a vital need for everyone, even grown-ups and that it is essential to their health and growth. Explain that a good night's sleep will make them feel happy, enthusiastic and alert and will help their memory and performance at school so they won't be so grumpy and tired in the morning.

I also think it's helpful to remember to follow your own boundaries and rules – there's no point in insisting that your child eats all their vegetables if you just tuck into your chips and leave your carrots! Or if you deny them TV time while you sit and devour your favourite soap. You do have to walk your talk, as you are a role model all the time whether you like it or not. So by taking back control of your parenting you are doing your child a great service and helping them learn how to negotiate the world, stay safe and keep out of trouble, and learn the vital skill of facing the consequences of their actions.

Discipline is really all about getting along with others and learning how to regulate, control and conduct yourself in different situations. Getting your kids to behave is not about harsh words, Dickensian punishments or alienating yourself from them – it's about creating a healthy loving environment, respectful discipline and setting boundaries because you love your children.

Boundaries: The Sheep in a Field Analogy

When I was in Teaching Training College many years ago, I saw a cartoon with some sheep in a field – it was a great analogy for kids about discipline and it has stayed with me ever since. I hope you'll also find it helpful and thought-provoking.

Imagine you are a sheep in a field with a really tight pen, where the boundary fence is too close to you and you are hemmed in and smothered. Imagine how you feel.

Now imagine you are a sheep in a vast field where there are no boundaries at all around you – there is no sense of security from danger and no one protecting you and keeping you safe, or even caring about what happens to you. You are frightened and out of control. Imagine how that must feel.

Finally, imagine you are a sheep in a pen where you can walk around, sometimes make decisions for yourself but can't stray too far. You have a flexible but sturdy fence around you that moves a little bit further out as you get older, more mature and independent. It isn't too close for comfort and it allows you to bounce against it sometimes to test its strength, but it stands firm and solid, protecting you and always with your best interests at heart because it loves you. It makes you feel safe, nurtured, loved and respected. Imagine how that would feel.

So – which field would you rather be in? What sort of fence are you creating for your kids at the moment?

Now imagine you are stepping into your child's view of the world.

- What do you notice?
- What sort of things do you hear?
- What are you aware of from this perspective?
- What have you learnt about yourself as a parent from doing that exercise?

As parents, we all create fences around our children to keep them safe but it's helpful to detach sometimes and to step back from what we do unconsciously so that we can become aware of the messages we are sending our children with the fences we have put round them.

By detaching, we can analyse if we are being over-protective, over-controlling or too laissez-faire in our approach as our children mature. We need to be flexible and adaptable and notice whether fences need to be moved as our children grow up and need different things from us.

What Could You Do Differently?

This book is not intended to make you beat yourself up or feel like a lousy parent. In fact it's meant to achieve the very opposite – it's about you building up your confidence, developing your skills and being brave enough to try new things. So instead of feeling guilty if you discover that you don't like what you're currently doing, just ask yourself: 'What small changes could I make this week or do differently this week in terms of discipline?' Could you be more assertive, could you speak in a firmer tone, or look more serious when you are telling your kids off? Go over in your mind some small changes you could make this week that will make a real difference in your discipline over time.

Emulate someone who has good discipline with their children

I want you to think about someone you know who disciplines their kids easily and naturally, and to notice what are they doing that you could copy. This is called 'modelling' and is a fantastic tool to add to your toolkit of parenting skills. The person doesn't need to know what you're doing – and because they are already good at it you are saving yourself a lot of time and anguish in making an easy, effective change. So go on, try it for this week and notice what they are doing, what they are saying, how they are standing, what their eyes are doing, how they hold their body, the tone of their voice and the words they use. Do they speak slowly and clearly? Do they wait for their kids to do as they ask? Simply observe them closely and then copy the sort of things they are doing with your own kids and see what happens.

Your Changing Role as a Parent

Let's break down your role as a parent into three stages, which should give you a new perception on what it means to be a parent:

Your kids are aged 0–6 years: the teacher role

The first six years of parenting are like being a teacher. You teach your children how to handle a beaker, a knife and fork, how to go to the loo, open doors – everything they need to know to survive in life and make sense of their world. At this age, children imitate. They literally absorb life around them, so we can never be too kind, too respectful, or too patient with them as we are their primary and most influential role models and they are learning from us all the time. This is usually a stage that parents really enjoy despite how tired they feel, as it is so exciting to watch your child walk, talk, read and make friends.

Your kids are aged 7–12 years: the manager's role

At ages six to seven, a child moves from 'learning to read' to 'learning to learn' and you become like an administrator or manager in their lives. They look to the wider world to learn about life and their circle becomes more social. This is setting the stage for the teenager to come. So look at how you handle discipline, discussions and respect as this is your training ground for the next stage to come.

Your kids are aged 13+ years: the coach

When a child hits around 13 years, something extraordinary happens: the cognitive abilities develop and they are able to understand more abstract thought processes. They become unsure of themselves and their hormones kick in. They start thinking for themselves and trying to develop their own independence. This is when a new style of communication is needed and, as a parent, you adopt more of a supporting role. Managing and teaching in a nagging, criticising, blaming, threatening tone really doesn't help. You need to manage yourself first, so that you can then support your teenager through the changes.

Common Types of Discipline

We are all naturally very different in the way we react to our children. Some of us are very strict while others are relaxed and easy-going. It's not for me to judge your style, but I do think it's helpful and useful to be aware of your style and the influences upon it, so that you can adapt, tweak or change it if you are not happy with the messages you are sending or teaching your children.

We are all enormously influenced by our own experiences and I work with many parents who react against the way their own parents disciplined them. For example, I worked with a lovely mum who had two small children and she was having problems with her three-year-old when she had another baby. We looked at what was causing her to feel so overwhelmed and tired and why her three-year-old was misbehaving at bedtimes, and she suddenly had a 'Eureka Moment' when she said, 'Oh no, I am a pushover!' She burst into tears as she said she didn't want to be as harsh, unforgiving and critical as her father had been with her. We worked at finding a new balance between the two very different styles so that she could relax and feel more in control of her discipline in a more confident way.

You may discover in this chapter that memories from your past help explain what's going on at the moment; this doesn't mean you need to blame your parents for your style, you just need to be aware of their influence on your style of parenting now and change it if you don't like what you are currently doing.

Here are some of the common parenting styles that most parents fall into:

The authoritarian parent

If this is your style of parenting, then your children are expected to follow your strict rules without question and you get angry if they don't. You often forget to explain the reasoning behind your rules and you hear yourself saying, 'Because I said so.' It's great that you have high expectations, but if you expect your instructions to be obeyed without explanation you can come across to your children as inflexible and rather heavy-handed in your approach. You may also find that you make things worse, as you often hit power struggles with your kids.

If you recognise that this might be your style, ponder what your children are learning from you and ask yourself: 'How will my children describe me to their children one day? Will my children resent me as I seem rather inflexible? Do I need to explain the reasoning behind my expectations so that my children understand my intentions?'

These questions will allow you to look at the longer-term, bigger picture of your style of discipline and may help you to decide if this is the style that you want to continue with.

The laid-back, chilled-out parent

Parents who felt too controlled as a child often react to their own childhood experience by giving their children very few, if any, boundaries. If you are what's known as a 'Permissive Parent', you may be rather indulgent with your children and you probably make very few demands on them. You may find that you rarely discipline them because you have relatively low expectations of maturity and self-control for them. You may feel that you have lost control of your child and you may hear yourself saying, 'Well, what's the point – they'll do what they want anyway.' You are probably not very demanding in your approach to discipline and perhaps other people see you as quite lenient, as you prefer to avoid confrontation. You are very nurturing and kind and get on well emotionally with your children but you may find that you are taking on the status of a friend more than that of a parent.

Children of this discipline often feel ill at ease or insecure as they have nothing to push against and can feel abandoned and unloved deep down. They also don't do as they are told quickly and may have problems conforming at school. You may find that you are exhausted a lot of the time and feel your kids aren't listening to you. This is when some children start getting into trouble, or start doing things to get your attention or really push your limits to see how far they can go.

If you believe that this is your style, contemplate what your children are gaining from it. Ask yourself: 'How will my children describe me to their children one day? Do my children need me to be their parent or their friend? What messages am I sending if I am too lenient with them – what are they learning?'

The uninvolved parent

If you have an uninvolved parenting style then you'll find that you make few demands on your children and that you get a poor reaction to your discipline and little effective communication with them. You naturally take care of your kids but you are generally detached from your child's life. You may be tired, exhausted or suffering from depression and you may find that your children tend to lack self-control and have low self-esteem.

Consider what your children are learning from you if this is your style of discipline and ask yourself: 'How will my children describe me to their children one day? How can I get more involved and interested in my child's life? How can I talk, chat and have fun with my kids more? How can I build up and increase my own confidence?'

If your parenting style is strained due to exhaustion or depression, then do seek help to try to work through this problem. Discuss any troubles with your family and friends and try to come up with practical solutions for reducing your load and giving yourself more relaxation time in your day. If you think you are suffering from depression then seek advice from your GP.

The balanced, fair and flexible parent

The other sort of discipline, which is the one you may want to aim for, is to be balanced, fair and flexible, and it means being clear about your expectations and always handling the same behaviour in the same way – this is my preferred style and the one I try to use with my own kids. This style strikes a balance between having a clear structure with clear expectations but also allowing you to be flexible, because life with kids isn't an exact science! This style allows for your kids to have some say in what they can and can't do as they get older, and helps them take responsibility for their own behaviour. Your children know that you are in charge and they know when they have gone too far, as you show, teach and explain to them where your limits are.

If this is your natural style, you probably find that you ask your children questions to help them think for themselves and you forgive rather than punish them harshly, but you also expect your kids to learn from their mistakes as it is important to you for your children to learn to self-regulate as well as be co-operative. This style gives room to grow and make mistakes, but everyone understands the general rules and limits on behaviour. And you probably feel confident in your parenting and believe in teaching your kids your values while having realistic and flexible expectations of them. It's likely you are firm, fair and flexible – but most of all consistent.

This parenting style tends to result in children who are happy, capable and successful, according to Diana Baumrind (who conducted a study of more than 100 pre-school-age children in 1967). If you recognise this style as your own, ponder what your children are learning from you and ask yourself: 'How will my children describe me to their children one day? What are my children learning about themselves from my style of discipline?'

Loving Discipline

Experts talk a lot about 'loving discipline' but what is it exactly? Loving discipline is a combination of telling your kids what behaviour, values, principles and rules are important to you and ensuring that they abide by them. It involves training, teaching and talking to your children and surrounding them with firm, fair and consistent boundaries, not only punishing them. It's about caring enough to say 'no' to your kids, something that many parents seem to find difficult. It means being respectful, calm, kind and compassionate but also in charge of your child's behaviour; setting clear boundaries according to your child's age, maturity and character and teaching them about choices and consequences.

It is not about shouting, nagging, dominating, controlling, threatening, giving harsh criticism, being violent or out of control, but instead being relaxed, positive and clear about your own expectations and noticing and praising when your kids are doing something right. All this will encourage them and keep them hopeful and on track. It's really all meant to teach your children responsibility and self-discipline, so that they grow up happy, well balanced and self-regulating.

Your children need you to be a leader and role model more than a friend and they need you to give them positive attention, not just shout at them, swear at them, threaten or frighten them in order to control them.

Daydream Yourself to Success

I want you to relax, and take in some slow, deep breaths – and imagine a time when things have gone really smoothly and well with your kids.

- What are you seeing?
- What are you saying?
- How are you feeling?

Make the picture brighter and closer to you and see what your kids are doing.

Hear what your kids are saying.

And imagine how your kids are feeling when it's all going well.

Bring this picture still closer to you and make it even brighter – turn up the sharpness to high definition and make the sounds louder and clearer and the intensity of the feelings stronger; squeeze your right hand into a fist to remind yourself of this lovely moment.

Now imagine a time in the near future when things are going really well – you are in control of your kids' behaviour, you have firm boundaries in place and everyone feels much happier, more secure and more relaxed in each other's company.

- See what you would see.
- Hear what you would hear.
- Feel how you would feel.

Really enjoy these feelings of being relaxed and in control – knowing you are doing the right thing for your child in the long run.

Keep breathing deeply because when you are relaxed everyone around you relaxes and life is much easier and more harmonious. Let your imagination and unconscious mind start to think about some small changes that you could make this week that would make life with your kids easier and more structured, and where you are very clear in the behaviour that you want to see from your kids – where you expect them to do as you ask, where you don't plead, beg or shout at them. Where you stand firm – planted firmly in the ground like an oak tree or like an anchor deep down on the bottom of the sea – unmovable, unshakeable, unflappable. Where you know that by you being a rock of dependability your kids are learning the wonderful gift of self-control.

Now imagine a time when there are some challenges thrown in – things aren't quite working out as you imagined, it's not quite going to plan, things are a bit pear-shaped or unpredictable – and imagine yourself handling the situation with ease, control and flexibility, or with humour and with confidence.

- See what you would see.
- Hear what you would hear.
- And feel how you would feel.

Continue to breathe easily and deeply, and relax around those challenges; imagine it all going perfectly and relax even further, knowing that you can handle whatever life throws at you easily, effortlessly and successfully.

Now come back into the present moment and bring all the wonderful learning and resources of that experience with you and remember that you can create these feelings of control and success by squeezing your right hand into a fist any time you need some support and grounding when disciplining your kids.

Consistency: The Magic Ingredient to Success

Another key skill to develop as a parent, being consistent is one of the simplest, yet most important strategies for successful discipline. Your consistency really is the key to success – every time your child pushes the perimeter fence of your boundary, push back, making your limits crystal clear. Give a sanction, take away a privilege, or reward the good behaviour, but keep your message consistent. It's really important – your kids will eventually get the message that you mean what you say.

Be clear about your expectations and always handle the same behaviour in the same way. It's the key to a warm and positive relationship between your kids and yourself. For example, if your child throws his toys at another child who's come round to play and you say 'no' firmly, then remove them from the toys for a few minutes, they'll get the message and make the connection over time if you keep doing the same thing. But if you say 'no' one minute then say, 'Oh, all right then,' because you're tired or chatting with your friends, your child picks up a mixed message.

Consistency in discipline really is the way to encourage good behaviour in your child. Many parents worry about their styles of discipline and punishment, but your most important disciplinary tool is consistency. It doesn't matter if you use a star-chart system, time-out in their bedroom, banning the TV or PlayStation, or even resort to bribery, as long as your rules and expectations are delivered consistently. If you are suddenly having a difficult time disciplining your child, take a step back and consider inconsistency as a possible first reason.

Look at your levels of stress, as this is the key area that causes inconsistent parenting. If you are going through a change, like divorce, a house move or a new job, you may be more distracted and unpredictable. Keep to your usual routines. That tends to help the rhythm of your home and helps your child feel safe, secure, in control, and therefore still self-confident. Maintaining a united front as parents is certainly desirable, as children up to 11 tend to see the world in black and white. During the teenage years, however, children understand that people can disagree and have differences.

On important decisions and principles, make sure you and your partner have talked through your point of view privately and support each other. Parenting is not a competition between you. Just remember to always do the right thing for your child.

Let's look at why it's often hard to be consistent.

Defending your boundaries

All of us find discipline hard at times – we might be tired, too busy, lacking confidence, feeling guilty, confused about what's really acceptable behaviour, or we might find it all too much hassle or want to be liked. You may even be reacting to the way you were disciplined as a child, or your partner may not support you in the way you'd like.

But if we don't do it as parents, who will?

Consistency avoids confusion because your children know how you are going to react and it gives them a sense of security and familiarity. But being consistent takes energy. Sometimes you may be tired, in a bad mood or busy and feel like letting your kids 'get away with it', but over time this will erode your authority and then you can over-react to something minor and everyone gets confused and upset. Your job is to guide, nudge and steer your kids in the right direction, but it requires lots of hard work if you are to really succeed, so you need to have lots of energy, be very clear about what is and isn't acceptable to you and stay centred when they cry, shout, sulk or throw a tantrum (no matter what their age). You have to remember that your mother-in-law, neighbours, family, friends, your children's teachers and society as a whole will thank you for raising well-behaved children, not monsters or aliens! With a positive attitude and a clear awareness of the rules, your kids will also thank you later…honestly!

I've already used this analogy but I want to remind you of it because I think it's a good one: remember that an aeroplane is off course for 90 per cent of its journey and needs constant gentle adjustments to keep it on course to arrive at its destination safely. Think of your kids as the aeroplane, needing a gentle nudge in the right direction, a gentle word, a guiding hand, not a nagging, criticising, judgemental, shouting voice. It's a tough experience, growing up.

One of the biggest frustrations of being a parent is the daily struggle to get our kids to behave in ways that are acceptable to us and to society. A great deal of parenting energy goes into getting them to take a bath, to say 'thank you', hang up their clothes, do their homework or to help around the house. We want courtesy, cleanliness, order and routines and they couldn't care less! The more we insist – the more they resist. But you always need to have the bigger picture in your mind.

I think it's really helpful to know and to remember these facts:

- **Fact 1:** Your children need to know how far they can go.
- **Fact 2:** Knowing your boundaries makes your kids feel secure.
- **Fact 3:** Boundaries keep your children safe.
- **Fact 4:** Boundaries teach your children to respect other people and other people's property.
- **Fact 5:** Boundaries teach your children self-control.
- **Fact 6:** Boundaries help your children develop into responsible adults.

What will you not put up with?

Many parents that I work with feel they should instinctively 'know' how to control or manage their child's behaviour, that somehow it should be 'natural' to them. Well, my strapline is 'kids don't come with a handbook'. Most parents have never had to manage another person's behaviour before – and even if they have through their work, it's not usually a child's behaviour. Children are a law unto themselves. There is a reason why actors say, 'Never work with animals or children'!

Stop now and write down a list of the things that are absolutely not acceptable to you as a parent (perhaps you could do this with your partner, too, so that you're both going in the same direction) – try not to make the list endless as it can be too controlling and restrictive, but be very clear on things that you will definitely not accept: for me it's spitting, biting, swearing and physically hurting.

You already have a set of values that you learnt about in Chapter 1, and now you have a list of things that are really not okay. This enables you to be completely clear about what is and what isn't acceptable to you, so that life gets easier. It helps you to conserve your energy for the important issues.

Let's do another exercise.

How Your Children See You

Relax, breathe deeply and slowly and ask yourself these questions:

- How do my children see me? As a friend, authority figure, disciplinarian, teacher, carer, partner or equal?
- Am I happy with their perception of me?
- Am I different or similar to my parents?
- Do I want to make some small changes to improve or fine-tune my discipline?
- What could these changes be?

What did you discover and learn about yourself from doing this simple exercise? Are these the messages you want your child to have about you? What small changes can you make this week to help start a new process?

Understanding Your Child's Behaviour

There is **always** a reason why kids behave in the way they do. There is a reason why your child is well behaved, just as there is a reason why they are behaving badly, and kids misbehave for a number of reasons:

1. To explore
- To test things out
- To see what response and reaction they get from you
- To copy the example you set for them

When young children are being curious and trying to increase their understanding of the world, it can come across as them being 'naughty'. For example, if a young child picks up a glass vase, they are probably just interested in its brightness and sparkle – they don't understand that they could break it or hurt themselves.

2. Looking for limits

Throwing something on the floor for the eighth time or coming in later than their curfew are all the same in terms of your kids testing your limits. So be very clear what is acceptable to you and stick to your guns.

> **Choose your battles. Don't fight every battle because, long term, you could lose the war!**

3. Boredom, attention-seeking and wanting your time

The third possible reason for poor behaviour is boredom and attention seeking. All children want your attention and a bored child will often start misbehaving just to get it. Don't make the BIG mistake of rewarding this sort of behaviour as you will reinforce the bad behaviour that you want to avoid.

Of course, it is really difficult to ignore infuriating behaviour like this. As a teacher I had to work hard not to give the 'naughty' children all my attention, but through my training with Jenny Mosley, who introduced the 'Quality Circle Time Model' into hundreds of schools, I learnt to reinforce only the really positive behaviour by giving lots of praise to a child who did exactly as I wanted. It's tiring at first and requires you to change the way you think but it can be very effective. Try catching your child doing something well and immediately say something like: 'Well done for getting your homework out and making a start on it before I had to remind you,' not, 'I see you've got your books out but I don't see much work being done.'

Do be aware of the signals that you send, because you are the main role model for your child. You are constantly demonstrating the right way to behave with a variety of other people, and your children will observe the way you talk, the words you use; your body language and how you react to different types of behaviour. So if you shout loudly at your child, but then tell them off for shouting themselves, what sort of message is that? That only adults are allowed to shout?

When you demonstrate the behaviour you do want from your kids, you can watch the massive improvements happen. Be patient – they will.

4. Unhappiness
Your child may not be mature or experienced enough to recognise when they are tired, hungry, in a bad mood or unwell, and they may simply whinge, whine or 'play up'. As an adult, you should be able to recognise the signs and make allowances for them. Still be clear about what behaviour you'll accept, but stay more flexible until they feel better.

A number of different foods and additives have been linked to bad behaviour in children but the research is controversial; however, it's just common sense to give your kids a healthy diet with lots of fruit and vegetables and to keep them away from fizzy drinks and sugary snacks.

Are your children motivated towards a goal or away from a problem?

This is my secret weapon in helping parents discipline their children. Once you have cracked your child's code for motivation you have mastered the way to discipline them in the way that is most effective for **them**!

Start to notice what already works with your kids – ask yourself whether your children are motivated **towards** pleasure, rewards and fun, like treats, extra play time or extra stories, or **away from** painful things or missing out, like not being allowed to watch their favourite TV programme, losing their computer time or being grounded from play dates for a week. Once you have cracked their motivation you have cracked your discipline problems.

Being 'toward' motivated will make your child feel as though they are being moved or pulled towards a goal and will encourage the 'I can't wait to get there' kind of feeling in them. Your child will have a positive feeling about moving towards success and you can use it to motivate them towards the behaviour you do want to see. Research proves that 'toward' motivation gets more consistent results over time than 'away-from' motivation.

There may be three potential problems if your child is too 'away from' motivated:

1. They may only take action when things get really bad.

2. There's more stress associated with getting the behaviour you do want to see as it's more challenging and negative.

3. Your child is not learning to take responsibility for their behaviour in the long term and may lose motivation for behaving well unless you quickly set up something they can aim for that motivates them personally.

I think you need to work out what works best for each of your children. Here are some thoughts for you to contemplate:

- Different sanctions work best for different types of children – going to bed early might be a sanction for one child but a reward for another.

- Some other sanctions could be: sitting on a step, going to their room, losing time on the computer, being grounded, missing a party or a favourite programme or whatever really 'gets' to your child. Think about what might work in your home.

- Some kids are motivated towards something, whereas some kids are motivated away from things – so think about each of your children and work out which style they prefer.

- It's a good idea to remember that children are constantly changing and what works well one day may not work the next.

- One key skill you must develop is that if you threaten a sanction you must carry it out, otherwise you send a message that what you say doesn't really matter and you lose your credibility and authority. If you carry out your sanctions clearly and quickly, your child will know you mean what you say and will think twice the next time before doing the same thing.

- Try to keep your own emotions out of the situation, as when you are angry or hurt you don't deal with the situation rationally or at your best.

- Don't make it personal – blame doesn't help the situation.

- The best sanction is often just a stern look of disapproval as it shows your displeasure or disapproval and is a very powerful message to most children.

Also remember to match the punishment with the crime and don't overdo it!

It's the traditional carrot-and-stick scenario but once you have discovered your own child's preference you can work with it to get the behaviour you do want from them and to teach them to make better choices.

How To Get The Behaviour You Want

There are two approaches to getting the behaviour you want:

1. Encouragement
2. Punishment

As a teacher I found that getting kids to co-operate was often easiest with praise. A lot of parents forget this, as they get caught up in the negative feelings caused by their child's poor behaviour. The best and most effective strategy long-term is the use of encouragement or what I call Positive Parenting. If you expect the very best behaviour from your children you will get it – it's called a self-fulfilling prophecy. Try to create a positive rather than a negative atmosphere in the relationship between you and your children. Learn to focus on the good behaviour and to praise and reward quickly, and try to send at least three rewards to every punishment to keep the emphasis on the positive approach to your discipline.

Rewarding good behaviour

There are four different types of rewards:

1. Praise

Praise is a powerful reward, as it makes your kids want to please you. It is one of the easiest rewards to give, and because it makes your child feel good, it also develops their self-esteem. So be liberal, generous and sincere with your praise and be very specific in what you praise your child for (see more on page 164 about praising your child specifically).

2. Treats

Treats such as sweets and extra TV are very popular, followed by money with older children. But I think treats work better if you use them as a privilege rather than a 'right'. There can be many types of treat because you know your own child best; so it could be staying up a bit later, playing outside for longer or having an extra story read to her.

> **Different rewards work better at different ages, and different rewards work better for different children. Bear in mind though that rewards only work if your child values them and actually wants to receive them.**

3. Time

As a reward, spending some 'quality time' with their parents can be a powerful motivator for kids, but it is not always the first reward parents think to use. It's free, it's fun and it doesn't have to be educational. It can be playing a game, going to the park; watching TV together or sharing an ice cream. Spending time playing, chatting and being together can be a huge treat and reward for your child. It doesn't have to be over the top.

4. Stars and stickers

Stars and stickers can be earned by kids over time and built up; they're an obvious way for your children to see evidence that they've earned your approval. There are some great stickers in the shops and they are perfect for most kids, especially younger ones, but beware of taking stickers away for bad behaviour as it can send out a negative message and demoralise some children.

Stickers are meant to be fun and positive and by giving a little reward or prize after achieving a certain number of stickers, kids feel very proud of themselves as it shows them visually how they are progressing and succeeding and motivates them even more to please you.

Make it clear why the reward is being given, with a clear connection between the good behaviour and the reward. Be clear about the goal that your child can aim for next time and always keep your expectations high.

Teach your child about consequences

Children need to learn to self-regulate so that they grow into responsible, independent, well-rounded individuals and to learn that their behaviour has consequences and they can influence an outcome by the choices that they make – even from when they are very little. So look for ways to teach your children about self-restraint and making better choices within your boundaries and rules, and empower your children with the long-term gift of self-control and autonomy.

It's important, regardless of the age of your children, to teach them the important lesson of consequences. If you only ever punish your child and don't explain why they have got into trouble or the consequences of their actions, your kids will find it hard to learn to take responsibility for their actions.

When I was teaching, we focused on the behaviour of the child, not the child themselves, and took time to explain about the consequences of doing what they had done. It takes a bit longer sometimes, but it is really important if you take the longer-term view.

The ability to say 'NO!'

Parents often find it hard to say 'no' to their kids and there are lots of reasons for this. One of the reasons is shortage of time. When you're in a hurry, it's much easier to relent and give your child what they want, rather than spending time telling them why they can't have it or having to negotiate their bad mood when they don't get it. But is that a message you want your child to grow up learning…expecting always to get their way?

Another reason is being afraid of causing a scene. Nobody wants to drag a screaming child round the supermarket while attempting to do their shopping! But distracting them with treats or snacks isn't the only answer – personally I think you can make looking for Postman Pat spaghetti hoops quite exciting, and getting your child involved in helping you look for something or helping you to weigh the fruit can be good practical experience and fun. It's how you approach it.

Be creative and try making chores or errands into a game – get your child to join in, not whine – get them engaged and also make sure that your kids aren't hungry or thirsty or over-tired as these factors will always affect how they behave when you are trying to negotiate shopping or rather mundane everyday activities. Also play games that get your children thinking when they are waiting at the petrol station or sitting in a restaurant or waiting for the dentist to see them. The old favourite 20 Questions is a great game to get inquisitive minds focused on something that distracts them from their boredom. The game begins with one person choosing pretty much anything they can think of. The first question for the guessers is usually 'Animal, vegetable, or mineral?' though it doesn't have to be. Players then go through a litany of questions trying to work out the nature of the mystery object and answers can only be 'yes' or 'no'. The winner is the person who guesses the object first or can stump the other players with their object.

Another reason why parents find it hard to say 'no' is all the resources available to us nowadays. When your child asks for a treat you may think, 'Well it's only cheap, so it can't hurt,' but even if you have plenty of disposable cash to spend on your children, what message are you sending out to them by buying everything they want and continually 'giving in'? That they can have anything they want? This approach is helping your child develop totally unrealistic expectations of you and the world in general – they will expect to get everything they want and no doubt their desires will get bigger and more expensive as they get older. It's Lego today; designer handbags tomorrow! Although indulging your child may make you feel good, you are setting them up for a huge shock when they can't get what they want in the real world. There may be big disappointments in store for them.

You are also sending out the message that no matter how they treat their things – they can always get more. Children who constantly get new toys and treats too easily learn not to value their things, because they know that they will always be replaced. They lose their sense of awe and wonder for new things if they are continually showered with gifts. It all comes too easily, so they have inflated expectations and no sense of gratitude or value for any of the gifts or treats they receive. I remember my own mum getting cross with my kids at Christmas a few years ago, as they were so overwhelmed by the amount of presents they received from both sets of grandparents that they became nonchalant and blasé and she felt that they didn't appreciate what they had received and just ripped the paper off, moving too quickly on to the next present.

Ask yourself if this is you at the moment: 'I can't give you much time but I can give you lots of "things".' If this is the message your child is receiving don't be surprised if they don't place any value on these things or show any gratitude. 'Things' can't replace your time. Have a think about whether your children are getting the message that you're happy with. Perhaps your kids feel that they are not worth spending time with. So you might be giving your child lots of gifts, but taking away their self-esteem. Now there's a thought...

Do you always give your children a treat when they cry or get upset? This is a dangerous message to send out. The rest of the world will not be as generous as you, and your child will face a nasty surprise when they realise they most definitely won't always get their way in the adult world? It's a balance between 'yes' and 'no', and it takes practice if you are new to saying 'no' and taking a harder line.

Start saying 'no' when your child asks for things like sweets, toys and treats and only give them on special occasions. This will encourage your child to value gifts and treats much more. Cut them down gradually and appropriately – every family is different, so decide what is best for your family and agree to stick to it, and if your child is old enough, explain these new rules to them. Meanwhile, start saying 'yes' to requests for your time, and be sure to find and make that time. Parenting isn't about 'putting up with' your child. They will have grown up before you know it, so enjoy spending time with them doing things **they** like to do. Give them the choice of how they want to spend time with you. Discover their interests, let them show off their new skills and knowledge, praise them and encourage them while you chill out together.

Initially it may be difficult as your child may not understand that you really mean 'no', because this was never the case before. There will probably be a tantrum, but remember the bigger picture of your parenting – the values you want to instil – and think about the consequences of giving in. Distract, explain, smile or move on to something else, but stand firm.

Remember to think about what your child is learning when you say 'no' and you mean it, as you are teaching them a valuable and important lesson for life. Reflect on this each time you discipline your children: 'Is this teaching my child something I believe to be important?'

Discipline strategies that don't work

As well as understanding what does work when it comes to managing behaviour, it is also vital to understand what doesn't work. We all slip into our old bad habits when we are too tired to get it right and often this just makes the situation worse. So forgive yourself, but be aware of what you're doing.

- **The empty threat**
  Try never to threaten a punishment that you're really not going to use: this only weakens your position in the future and your children will learn not to trust you or believe you and most importantly not listen to you or heed your threats. I've heard lots of examples of this on my travels; things like: 'If you don't stop doing that *right this instant*, I'll stop the car, let you out, and you can walk home,' which I've heard said to a four-year-old, miles from home. Or, 'Okay, that's it – we're getting rid of the TV!' Or the most common one: 'If you don't pick up these toys, I'll throw them in the bin!'

- **Getting wound up**
  It's all too easy to lose your temper when your child is messing around, but anger is simply not an effective control strategy.

Take a deep breath, press your pause button, relax and realise what you're doing.

- **Being negative**
  Sometimes it takes an awful lot of energy to stay positive, but over time a negative approach will only make things far worse.

- **Being confrontational**
  When you're faced with an obstinate or confrontational child, stay calm; if you are aggressive, your child learns to be more aggressive themselves. If that's not an attribute you want to teach your child then learn to be less aggressive with them.

- **Getting pulled in**
  Getting drawn into arguments is a waste of your energy. If you set fair boundaries, you don't need to debate them. They are non-negotiable.

- **Backing your kids into a corner**
  Children don't understand how or when to back down. So if you learn to be flexible when it is necessary, you give your child a way out.

- **Beating yourself up**
  Be positive with yourself, as well as with your child: we all make mistakes, but it is the ability to learn from them that really matters so that you can move on in a positive direction.

All kids want to know how far they can go and will push your boundaries – it shows a healthy streak of independence and spirit too – but you need to push back at times and stand firm. Kids respect that and then you both know where you are.

My Top Tips for Disciplining Your Children

Here are my very simple steps to successfully disciplining your children easily and effectively.

- The first step is to **KISS** your discipline: **K**eep **I**t **S**hort and **S**imple!

  This little saying has helped transform hundreds of family lives over the years as many of the parents I've worked with have popped this saying on to a Post-it note in their kitchen to remind them that keeping rules short and simple helps kids remember them.

  Keep your rules Short and Simple

  Keep your language Short and Simple

  Keep your consequences Short and Simple

- **Be sure**

  Earlier in the chapter I asked you to write down exactly what you would and wouldn't accept from your child so that everyone in your family, including your partner, mother-in-law and childcarer, is really clear, certain and confident about the sort of behaviour you expect in your home. This gives your children security and clarity. Children brought up used to consistent discipline from all the adults around them are more confident and relaxed as they know what is expected of them. I have found that being vague stresses everyone out and sends really mixed messages to your children, and the higher your expectations for your children the better they will behave.

  I work with so many parents who simply forget to tell their kids what they expect from them and think that they will just pick their rules and expectations up by osmosis, but children need to be shown or told what is expected of them as they are not mind readers. So make sure you teach and tell your kids about your rules, expectations, choices and consequences so that everyone is sure, clear and certain.

Try this simple technique that breaks the usual pattern in the way you react so that your child will remember the lesson far more:

Be surprised rather than angry when things go wrong – it works wonders – and say something like: 'Oh gosh, I think you've forgotten our rule haven't you? Never mind – shall I remind you that we don't run down the stairs in case we fall down and bang our heads?' And then simply smile.

This will kindly, gently and consistently reinforce your rule and make sure that your child is really certain of your expectations.

● **Be confident**

As I've said, confidence is contagious and if you are confident, certain, positive and relaxed about what you want from your children they will sense that you mean what you say so are less likely to mess you about.

Over the years I've noticed that my secret weapon in making life with children more rewarding, more enjoyable and lots of fun is actually by first building up your confidence as a parent. As you start to feel more in control of your family life and relationships you send out more positive vibes and your children pick up on that and react more positively to you too. I often teach the parents I work with to 'fake it till they make it' and to just act more confidently and assertively in the way they speak to their kids, handling their body language and their tone of voice more assertively, as this simple technique works brilliantly with children, like a self-fulfilling prophecy. The more confidently you act, the more confident you become over time.

- **Be consistent**
  We've had a good look at consistency earlier but it means being clear about your expectations and always handling the same behaviour in the same way. It avoids confusion and gives your children a real sense of security and familiarity – this really is the magic ingredient to easily and successfully disciplining your children.

- **Be calm, composed and grounded**
  It takes a lot of practice to stand back from a situation and not 'lose it' as your child answers you back for the fourth time that day, and it can feel unnatural to stay calm and not shout, can't it? Of course it's perfectly natural to lose your temper from time to time as kids need to know when they have gone too far, but it's also helpful to have some simple ways to stay calm, grounded and composed when it does all go 'pear-shaped'.

  Remember to press your imaginary 'pause' button when you're confronted with a tired or grumpy child or a completely messed-up bathroom and ask yourself, 'What is it I need to say now to move this situation forward positively for us all?' As an adult it's up to you not to lose your self-control completely because you can frighten, confuse, or encourage another repeat performance if your child really enjoys winding you up. It is also really bad for your long-term health to be overwhelmingly stressed by your kids' behaviour.

  The advantages of staying calm are that you can deal with the situation far more effectively and that you are setting a good example and being a great role model to your kids. You are really teaching them about self-control, which is a very important life skill to learn for adulthood.

A way to really gain control over your emotions is to think of the situation as ultimately your child's problem because they are not yet mature, grown-up or emotionally developed enough to act responsibly. This simple reframing of the situation shifts your perception to correcting them and teaching them and helps you move away from blaming them, which can build up resentment and anger in you – and that will only increase your stress levels.

- ## Be caring and considerate

Being caring means listening to your kids, talking with them, spending time together, giving hugs and providing a safe and secure environment for them, but it's also about remembering how it feels to be a child and putting yourself in your child's shoes sometimes and imagining life from their point of view. It means lightening up, being playful and having fun too. It's remembering that childhood is a special and magical time in a child's life and it should be a time of laughter, joy and discovery. So it's finding time for a cuddle and a laugh, listening when we are tired or bored with the story and finding ways to show our children that we care about them enough to spend time with them.

Being caring is also not allowing your kids to run riot by being ineffective and too lenient. We all care about our children, love them unconditionally and adore them but we also have a responsibility to teach them the rules, either the rules of your home, the rules of their school, the rules of our community or the rules of our society as a whole, so you need to prepare, teach and guide them to live in the BIG world, and caring means tough love sometimes.

But it's also about treating your child with care and consideration to their feelings, which may be very different to our own. You may shout because you are tired but they may not understand and may feel really hurt by your words or attitude. Just imagine you were at work and you did something foolish or got something wrong through inexperience and someone shouted at you – how would you feel?

So try to speak to your child with respect and show you care by being mindful and gentle because sometimes we lose sight of who the most important people are in our lives.

- **Be imaginative**

  My approach to parenting is to relax and think of new ways to relate to your children, constantly improving, fine-tuning and tweaking your techniques, strategies and approach. Why not make your own reward stickers, get messy together in the garden, or paint, draw or cook? Why not hit a cricket ball around in the garden or try to score a few goals at football between jumpers for goal posts? Why not shift your mindset and become a 'big kid' again? Train yourself to look for different ways to solve problems and also get your kids involved in coming up with ideas – it builds trust, connection and family bonds of respect and love.

- **Distraction**

  Another simple but really effective way to keep the atmosphere positive in your home is through distraction. Distracting a young child is a lovely way to keep them on track and to help them do as you want in a friendly, positive way (like saying, 'Oh come and look at this lovely butterfly,' while taking them away from pulling the petals off your favourite rose bush), but there will always come a time when you actually need to deal head-on with misbehaviour and disobedience. It's hard to know when you should move away from distraction to punishment but you'll know yourself when the time has come.

Expect some steps forward and some back, as we are all learning how to get along together and patience really is a virtue, but actually it's also a skill, a talent and a gift. We all know as parents that it can be hard to find patience some days, but forgive yourself if you get it wrong sometimes – we are all human – and be big enough to say you're sorry if you've lost it and said something you regret. It shows you are brave enough and confident enough to apologise.

The real challenge is to be patient when it's all going horribly wrong, but it's hard to be patient when your toddler has lovingly written all over the newly papered sitting room, or your 16-year-old has decided to cook chilli con carne but has left the mess for you to tidy up. The secret is pressing your 'pause' button, taking a deep breath and remembering the bigger picture once again – the relationship between you as a parent and your child. Try lightening up and seeing the funny side, and the pettiness and trivia of it compared to the really important things in life, and remember that they will soon have grown up and flown the nest and you'll miss the mess!

A successful parent is willing to try different things and keeps adapting, tweaking and fine-tuning their discipline until something works – they keep remembering the bigger picture, they stay firm and grounded and they always Keep It Short and Simple.

Managing your child's behaviour takes hard work, persistence, dedication, a sense of perspective and a healthy sense of humour but with time and effort you will succeed. Expect the best from your children, get the basics right, stay positive and they will grow up into well-mannered and well-behaved adults to make you proud.

Top Tips for Keeping it Simple

- Children need love, especially when they don't deserve it!
- You don't need to argue to be powerful.
- The key to successful discipline is simply being prepared.
- Be clear about what your rules and boundaries are.
- Make sure your kids know what these are.
- Be consistent in how you apply them.
- Be imaginative and curious in finding new and more effective ways to manage your kids as they are all different, unique and special.

5

Keeping Your Temper and Handling Conflict

Everyone gets angry with their kids at some time or another – it's normal, healthy and also inevitable because kids know just which buttons to push, and they push them! It helps to accept that anger is an honest emotion, but it's what you choose to do with your anger that's important.

Most people think their anger is justified at the time but it's often afterwards that many realise they have probably over-reacted and said or done things they regret. Anger that is expressed in an 'out-of-control' way can be dangerous and have serious consequences for the whole family because it can damage trust and create an atmosphere of fear.

However, don't be afraid to let your anger take its natural course because if you suppress it, this can lead to frustration, resentment, bitterness, stress, a sense of hopelessness and even depression, which is not a good thing for you or your children long-term. Getting angry doesn't make you a 'bad' parent. All children will misbehave and wind you up, but if you are having trouble handling your anger on a regular basis, then it might be time to notice what your triggers are and what causes you to lose your temper to see if there is a pattern to it so that you can pre-empt the flash points.

Let's take a look at your triggers.

Top Temper-tantrum Triggers

The common things children do that annoy parents the most are:

- Being rude or shouting at their parents
- Fighting with their siblings
- Not saying 'please' or 'thank you'
- Keeping their bedrooms untidy or leaving mess around the house
- Not doing their chores or homework
- Not eating their vegetables or other food

It happens to us all. One minute we're having a great time and feeling on top of the world. We're calm. We're patient. We're fun. Then suddenly, without warning, we start to change. We feel our heart beating faster, our temper starting to rise, and suddenly we explode into the Incredible Hulk – the Parent from Hell. The trouble is – it wasn't even a major incident. You can't even remember why or what exactly made you snap. Welcome to what I like to call the 'Parent Losing the Plot Moment'!

There's a great line in a Prince song that goes: 'Act your age not your shoe size', which I think just about sums anger up. A parent tantrum is powerful. It is like a tornado. It is destructive. It needs controlling. It's a good idea to learn new ways to manage your anger, and understanding what makes you angry can help you handle it better. So think about what makes you lose the plot and become really angry. Stop now and write down your top-four triggers.

- Which one makes you feel worse than all the others?
- What's the reason for that?

When conflict occurs, we can choose to engage in battle, back off or negotiate. Our choice depends very much on how secure we feel, how much we hang on to power and how sure we feel of our own ground. But one thing is for certain: your loss of control may stop your relationship from deepening and developing with your children and may damage it. It can even stop your child from facing problems and dealing with them in an effective way, or encourage your child to manipulate you. But regardless of all of this, one thing is for sure – anger can damage everyone's self-esteem.

Issues Surrounding Your Anger

Often when parents are angry they use language that attacks their child as a person rather than the behaviour, and this damages relationships. They say things like, 'You never do...' 'You always...' 'You are so...'

Here are some useful questions to ask yourself:

- What's my child learning from the way I respond to them when I'm angry?
- How consistent are my boundaries and limits – am I being clear in how I express what I want?

Imagine a perfect situation where everything is going beautifully and you are in control of your temper – what are you doing, hearing and feeling? What is going well? Why is it going well?

Now ask yourself what you could do differently from what you are currently doing to reach this perfect scenario and to make an improvement in controlling your anger and your temper. Is it pressing your imaginary pause button, is it counting to 10, is it making sure you're not rushing, or over-tired or hungry? Really think about what you can do to step back – away from the situation – and be more detached.

Now ask yourself what's stopping you making those changes.

Stress and anger are closely linked so think of ways to reduce your stress like having some 'me time' away from your children, finding someone to talk to, taking some form of physical exercise like walking the dogs or going out in the garden for 10 minutes to cool off.

Be patient with yourself as you learn new ways to cope with anger and stress – it takes time to form a new habit. But also reward yourself with little treats to celebrate your successes every day – a bubble bath with candles, a fresh cup of coffee, flowers or a magazine, and celebrate your baby steps towards happier relationships. Forgive yourself if you slip back now and again – you're only human!

What Habitual Anger Is Really Telling You

Maybe you're a person who's been angry for a long time or for a major part of your life. I call this 'habitual anger' because you've got used to behaving in this way so it's become a habit. Habitual anger is trying to tell you something – so ask yourself some deeper questions.

- Why am I finding myself angry all the time?
- What am I doing to create these situations time and time again?
- What is it that's making me angry?
- Who am I really angry at?
- What do I believe about my life that causes all these frustrations?
- Is this the only way I can react to life?

- What could I do differently?
- How could I feel more in control of my life?

Habitual anger is not good for your body as it creates stress, tension and illness. So it's a great relief when you start to understand what's causing it and begin to make some small changes to help you feel more in control of your life generally.

How to Handle Anger Positively

How do you release your feelings of anger at the moment? If you don't like what you find, don't beat yourself up; the first step to changing things in your life is to notice them. Here is a series of techniques to help you keep calm and get back in control of your emotions.

Four Steps to Control Your Anger

1. **Stop:** Pause for a moment and cool off. Don't discipline your child while you are angry. I always say to my clients to 'Strike While the Iron is Cold!' so that you don't over-react, or regret what you say or do.
2. **Think:** Read the situation quickly. Try to determine what is really happening.
3. **Plan:** Form a plan. Evaluate the problem, have a purpose, set goals, think of alternatives.
4. **Act:** Carry out your decision.

One way to control your anger is to press your imaginary internal 'pause button' (like the one on your DVD player) and ask yourself, 'What exactly am I annoyed or angry about?' This helps you step back from the situation – getting you back in control and helping to calm you down. Imagine the remote control in your hand as it's a great way to remember to get back in control.

There are usually triggers that set anger off, like not feeling listened to, not feeling valued, when something isn't fair, when you feel frustrated, or triggers like the ones listed earlier in this chapter. You will probably discover that you get wound up by the same things over and over again. So start to keep an anger diary so you can identify your triggers. Is it when you are hungry and tired and running on empty just before dinner? Is it when you go into your daughter's bedroom for the ninth time to tell her to turn the music down?

What physical signs warn you that you are about to 'lose it'? Do you start to breathe faster, get a tense neck, does your face go red or do you feel like a volcano is about to erupt as it rises up your body from your tummy? By starting to recognise your physical signs you are again getting back in control and stepping away from the situation, which is much better. You can start saying to yourself, 'I'm getting wound up now but it's okay, I can handle it,' or 'I can feel my temper rising like a volcano, but if I remember to take deep breaths I can stay calm and in control.' You are becoming aware of your triggers.

When writing in your diary, think about:

- What were the physical signs that you noticed when you started to feel your temper rising?
- How did you feel at the time – what were your thoughts?
- Where were you when you lost your temper as this may help you to notice patterns?

- What happened immediately before you lost your temper?
- How do you remember to stop yourself from losing your temper completely?
- What could you do differently next time?

Ask yourself this empowering and useful question: 'What would I like to see happen in a perfect world?' to start focusing on a new solution to your frustration. Relax and breathe slowly and deeply – this takes the edge out of the anger. You need to focus very specifically on what it is you want to see happen. This gives you clarity and direction and helps you pass this on to your children who often don't understand what exactly it is you want them to do.

Also ask yourself, 'Is my attitude moving me closer to or further away from the relationship I want with my children long-term?' This question takes you immediately out of the mundane and humdrum to look at the bigger picture of your parenting. It immediately changes your perspective.

Another positive step to take is to talk openly and honestly to your child about how you are feeling, in ways such as:

- 'I'm tired of telling you this over and over again because I feel…'
- 'I'm angry with you because…'
- 'I'm hurt because you did…'

This teaches your child about empathy and immediately takes the emotional charge out of your frustration.

Read on for practical ways to manage your anger as well as some simple methods to release and diffuse it.

Anger-management strategies

If you feel like screaming and shouting at your kids then your own anger has probably been building up for a long time. A helpful strategy is to look in a mirror and imagine talking to your child as if they were looking at you in that mirror. Tell them exactly how you feel – speak truthfully – explain all the frustration, anger, hurt or disappointment. This should help to get things off your chest.

Some simple ways to release anger or pent-up frustration are to hit a pillow, bounce on the bed, hit golf balls in the garden, go to the gym, or go for a long, hard walk round the block to let off steam – I have even been known to go into a cupboard and have a good swear to myself! Do something physical (but safe) to release your charged-up emotions. Don't be reckless or dangerous to yourself or your child. Just step back, breathe deeply and slowly, find what suits you and experiment with it. Sometimes you may even make yourself laugh because you look or sound ridiculous – a great way to change your mood.

Many women, particularly mums, have been taught that to be angry is bad and unacceptable and that to lose your temper means you are a Bad Person or a Bad Parent. However, swallowing your anger is an unhealthy response as it turns inwards and makes you feel unhappy, helpless, stuck, depressed and generally out of control of your life.

Ask yourself these questions to determine how you are handling your own anger:

- How do you hold in or let out your feelings of anger, frustration, resentment or being overwhelmed?
- Do you blame and berate your kids for how you are feeling?
- Do you shout or swear?
- Do you give them the silent treatment, ignoring them when they are trying to talk to you?

Now that you have stepped back and detached and noticed your reactions, are you happy with the way you handle these difficult emotions? Are you happy with the messages you are passing on and teaching your children in the way you handle these common negative emotions? If not, don't beat yourself up, but make some small changes that will create a better blueprint for your children to learn from.

Your anger can serve a positive purpose and help you to find out what's really bothering you deep down. Just asking yourself, 'What am I so angry about?' will help you identify what you'd like to change. It's usually something small that can make a big difference in your life and help you move forward. Once you've expressed your anger about the behaviour that you don't like in your child, don't criticise them personally. Do your best to forgive your child – and yourself – have a hug, say sorry, learn the lesson from the experience and move on.

Helping children stay calm and deal with their anger safely

Our environment naturally affects our stress levels, mood and how susceptible we are to getting angry, and you can really help your child stay calmer by doing things like:

- Having a regular routine and making sure your child gets enough sleep
- Avoiding violent TV programmes, books and games
- Helping them deal with their worries and anxieties
- Not yelling or shouting at them
- Providing a healthy balanced diet without too many additives
- Keeping the noise levels down in your house
- Avoiding extreme heat
- Talking about what it feels like to be angry

Explore and experiment, and notice ways you can calm things down in your household and teach your children to use the 'I' messages – so that they have a structured pattern and strategy to help them express their anger healthily.

Here are some safe ways for children to deal with their anger safely:

- Go and punch a pillow or hit a boxing ball – it gets rid of tension and adrenaline safely.
- Do some physical exercise – ride a bike, kick a ball, run round the garden.
- Draw a picture of how angry you feel and even tear it up!
- Write a letter getting it all out of your system – even if you never send it – it feels great to release how you feel.
- Find your own space to cool down.

Be a Role Model

With my two teenage kids, I know first-hand about having a parent tantrum but it can be avoided by setting firm, fair, reasonable boundaries throughout their lives. Be a figure of authority in your own home – I can make my kids conform with just a withering look…but maybe that's a result of my years as a teacher! Kids need boundaries and society needs them to have boundaries.

Acknowledge that it's normal to lose your temper sometimes and find a strategy or technique that suits you to release it safely. You are a role model for your children in everything that you do, so teach them how to handle anger and frustration healthily and talk about it with them.

What better gift can you give your children?

Smacking

Smacking shows a lack of respect for your child and it can so easily get out of control and escalate. Also, where do you go from there in your discipline if it doesn't work?

You are a role model for your child – no matter how old they are – so is hitting out and hurting another really what you want to teach your kids long-term as a way to handle their anger? Many people argue that they were smacked as a child and it 'never did me any harm' but studies have shown that children who are consistently smacked and hit suffer low self-esteem and often turn to violence later in life to solve issues.

Managing Your Child's Behaviour Has a Lot to Do with Your Attitude

If you see your child's poor behaviour as a problem and something that just gives you stress and headaches, it will; but if you see their behaviour as a challenge, a growing expression of their independence and a chance for you to become a better parent and maybe a more patient person, then you'll have a different mindset and a more positive outlook from the start. You need to see your child's behaviour as challenging or difficult but not see your child as 'bad'. This really helps you to work with your child, not against them. It takes hard work, dedication and persistence to get your little angels or little aliens to behave and to learn what is and isn't acceptable in the world.

The 'I' Message Simple Strategy

Here is an easy and simple new strategy to explore and develop. Try changing your language from 'You', which puts the blame on your kids and builds barriers of resentment, to 'I', which means you are taking responsibility for how you feel and is a way of expressing your anger in a clear and more respectful way. This is a more assertive way to communicate and it also helps you to control your anger, stopping the situation from escalating or getting worse.

'I' messages let you say what you feel without hurting your child's feelings. The key points to remember to say are:

- I feel…when you…because…
- I would like…

For example:

- **I feel** angry / annoyed / fed up **when you** forget to ring me when you say you will **because** I can't fall asleep as I'm waiting up to hear from you.
- **I would like** you to always take your mobile with you and keep it turned on so I can contact you to make sure you're safe.

Use this strategy to teach your children what they need to understand from your anger and each time expand on the '**because**'. Be very specific on what you would like to happen next time so that you can all keep learning from the ups and downs of family life and the anger has a positive aspect to it.

Make sure your kids know and are clear about the 'Anger Rules' for your family – a good way is to sit down and discuss them and then get one of your kids to design a poster with the rules on so that everyone can see them.

Here's an example of one family's poster of rules about anger.

It's okay to feel angry but...
Don't hurt anybody
Don't hurt anybody's feelings
Don't hurt yourself
Don't damage property
Don't cover up the truth
And let's talk about it.

These ideas can be adapted for older children by using the concepts of:

- Respecting yourself
- Respecting others
- Respecting property
- Always getting into the habit of talking about things openly

Building the 'we' mentality

Building the 'we' mentality of a team atmosphere in your home life is one very important aspect for successful and happy families, and is a great way to overcome feelings of conflict. The 'we', rather than 'me', mentality is so important in a family. It builds trust, support, loyalty, love and helps boost security and self-esteem.

One way to build the 'we' mentality is to practise family traditions – it can be as simple as eating together on Sundays, watching football together or going on an annual holiday together. These traditions hold special significance to your family and create warmth, commitment and a family history with memories to last a lifetime.

Another way to build the 'we team' is to talk. Share dreams, feelings, hopes, fears, joys and sorrows. Listen to each other when you talk about your experiences and needs. Talk about rules and routines and develop habits of supporting each other. A stable family pattern will give you the strength and support to deal with all the difficulties you may encounter in life – divorce, bereavement, being made redundant, sickness or an accident. A strong family unit can withstand these trials as it bends, not breaks, through change.

Stop now and think about how you would build your team. What things do you do that create that family togetherness? Now think of some more ways that you could develop to bring that team spirit into your family even more. See what you'd be doing, hear what people would be saying and feel the great feelings of support that will surround you as you build up and really create a sense of 'our family'.

Stand Back and Look from the Wider Perspective

This exercise is a great one for shifting your line of thought and getting some quick solutions, by seeing life from another family member's point of view. Lots of parents tell me that this exercise has been really illuminating for their families, so why not try it and see if it can work its magic on your family?

Get four pieces of paper.

1. Write on the first piece of paper: 'My point of view'.

2. Then on the second write: 'My child's point of view'.

3. On the third write: 'My partner's point of view'.

4. Finally, on the fourth write: 'A detached person's point of view'.

Stand on each piece of paper – one at a time – and try to see the world through the eyes of that person. Do this very slowly and deliberately, and take your time, even though it may seem a bit weird at first. Imagine you're seeing in great detail what that person sees – see through their eyes completely and 'become' that person for a few moments. Hear in great detail what they hear – notice the sounds and the words that they hear, and then really feel how they feel – enter into their world completely and just relax and let your unconscious do all the work.

As you step separately on each piece of paper, let go of who you are and become each member of your family individually, seeing the world or the problem through their eyes and ears, stepping into their world and being open to discovering a completely different perspective on what you have been experiencing from your own perspective.

This exercise opens you up to respecting different family member's perspectives, which can help everyone to negotiate and learn to see the different sides to a story, niggle or problem. It can provide solutions rather than you all going round in circles of misunderstanding.

You will probably discover a whole new way of thinking about your relationship, problem or the current situation after doing this simple and powerful exercise. Looking at the world from another person's viewpoint really can help shift stuck emotions and ideas and is great fun to do with your children as they are less self-conscious and more open-minded to this style of working; it often helps everyone to develop the 'we' mentality we were talking about earlier.

Co-operation

Co-operation is the oil of family relationships. It helps families search for solutions and understanding even when things get difficult. This is a key skill in helping families towards more harmony. If a family is turbulent on the inside, how is it going to survive the storms raging outside in the big, wide world?

One important principle in helping families to get on better is to introduce the ethos of 'Are we all willing to search for a solution to this problem?' Now, I'm not claiming this is at all easy, and if you haven't tried it before it does take a shift in your thinking – particularly when your son is holding your daughter over the banisters by the hair because she borrowed his hair gel – but it does work in the long term. It focuses everyone on the win-win habit.

No one likes to lose and we've all heard, 'But it's not fair!', but this way of thinking helps the whole family focus on creating something new and better together. It actually helps the family bond together more effectively.

So now think how you can get your children and other family members to start focusing on what works well for everyone – in what ways can you help change their mentality to find solutions and answers to normal family life where everyone feels it's fair?

One way is how you speak to your kids in those tricky moments of dispute and argument, by asking them for solutions that seem fair:

- 'What do you think would be a fair thing to do here so that we all feel okay about what happened?'
- 'What would work so that we all feel better about this?'
- 'What can we do to find a solution to this problem together?'

Your kids, partner and you will probably find this difficult at first, but stick with it and notice the real change for the better in your family attitude to each other – even young children will surprise you with their ingenuity and sense of fairness.

I think it helps to understand that being a parent is not about being popular or giving into every little whim and fancy of your child but actually about making decisions where everyone appears to win – even if it doesn't always appear to your children like that.

The skill you need to develop in your children is the skill of brainstorming ideas to find a solution. Parents forget that children are not born with this type of wisdom and need your patience to learn different strategies.

> 'Too often we give children answers to remember rather than problems to solve.'
> ~ Roger Lewin

Create house rules and stick to them

This simple idea is designed to give your family a framework and something on which to positively focus everyone's attention. It is a great opportunity for your children to get involved and to feel that they are part of the whole decision-making process in your house. It's not meant to be a long and soul-destroying list but more an incentive to co-operate. All children come up with super ideas. I've seen families with older kids write:

- We don't take anything without asking the person first (T-shirts, trainers or even chocolate!)
- When we go out, we will say where we are going, and who with, and when we will be back.

- Bedrooms have to be tidied, vacuumed and dusted every Sunday.
- When friends come round we are responsible for tidying up the mess.

Sit down with your family this week around the kitchen table and have a chat about some of the ideas for setting up House Rules. Explain that you'd like to help the atmosphere in the house improve and run more smoothly and you'd like their input and suggestions. Ask each member of your family to think of at least one house rule and write them down. Then put them up somewhere where everyone can see them clearly and easily – maybe one of your children would like to design something on the computer to make the rules look nice. Then arrange another chat the following week at the same time to see how it's all going. (Regular times are always a good idea so that you don't forget to do it.)

The Art of Negotiation

It's difficult to communicate effectively with kids all the time, from toddler to teen, and with teenagers, learning to negotiate is a special skill all of its own – it's really worth learning.

You say, 'It's time for bed,' 'It's time to go,' 'It's time for homework,' 'It's dinnertime!' But your child says, 'Five more minutes.' You're tired of saying 'no' and tired of fighting. So what do you do? Give in? Blow up, shout, lose the plot? Or – negotiate?

Life with kids often involves negotiation, whether we like it or not, and negotiating with them can actually be a great learning experience for your children as they mature. If you don't negotiate, your children may not learn how to deal with conflicts constructively and confidently, and if you don't teach them how to work with you, they may never learn how to work with others. So teaching your children to negotiate is a key learning skill that can help you all be more flexible when the situation calls for it and seems appropriate.

But **negotiating with kids is often a challenging process** as you need to learn how to manage your own emotions and frustrations, and one very common problem I have noticed is that when emotions run high, negotiating skills drop dramatically. Before you enter into your next negotiation with your child (and that could be in five minutes!) here are some pointers for negotiating with your children.

Tips for negotiating

- **Start an agreement, not an argument**.
  Take a few minutes to phrase your requests so that your child can say 'yes'. Your child will listen more readily and be more open to doing as they are told if you phrase your idea in a way that appeals to your child's need for independence. If you say, 'Would you like to set out the table mats or the knives and forks?' you are more likely to get co-operation than if you say, 'Set the table NOW!'

- **Get your child involved**.
  If it's getting near bedtime, try saying, 'How many more minutes do you think it'll take you to finish your drawing and get ready for bed on time?'

- **Explain your point of view**.
  You could say, 'We have to leave George's house now because I have to make dinner.' Once you have explained what's happening and have given your child a little time to get used

to the idea, remain prepared for their response. If your child says, 'I don't care, I'm not hungry,' you might say, 'But I am and so is your brother and we need to get home now as everyone's getting hungry.' Remember: don't get drawn in – no match, no game!

- **Know that negotiation doesn't mean giving in**.
When you negotiate to buy a new car, or negotiate on holiday in the market, you're not giving in – you're bargaining. Keep in mind that negotiating is not about winning and losing. It's about finding a sensible compromise so that everyone can win.

- **Negotiate issues in age-appropriate ways**.
If your nine-year-old doesn't like broccoli, ask them, 'What vegetable would you like instead?' If your toddler isn't interested in eating, instead of arguing, get creative and make their dinner into the shape of a face with carrots sticking out of their mashed-potato ears – be relaxed, creative and humorous – it can work wonders.

- **Respond to criticism with a reasonable question**.
If your child tells you to stop nagging about brushing their teeth, tidying their bedroom or having a bath, try saying, 'When would you like to do it?' and give them a limited choice – e.g. 'Before or after your story?'

- **Take time to cool down**.
If your child is making you angry, go and jump about in the garden, count to 100, hit a pillow or swear quietly to yourself in a cupboard to get your frustration out and to give you all a bit of a breathing space.

- **Write down solutions**.

  Get your family together, perhaps at a mealtime, and appoint a secretary who makes a list of everyone's ideas. Discuss them openly but don't allow criticism of anyone's idea. Also consider doing your negotiation in writing. Writing notes to an older child, such as, 'Clean room at 6pm', might prompt more co-operation than nagging would.

- **Let your child win sometimes**.

  Pick your battles wisely and remember that changing your mind doesn't mean you're losing or weak. You might say, 'Okay, I agree with you. But let's make a deal that next time you will listen to me before blowing up.'

- **Remember, you have the final say**.

  You don't have to reach a complete consensus in any negotiation. Sometimes, somebody just has to make a decision. It's perfectly okay for you as the adult to make the final decision, as long as you have heard your children's points of view and tried to be fair. Children will come to respect you and your judgement; they may not like it, but they will come to realise that it's fair.

There are times to negotiate and times not to negotiate. None of us has time to negotiate every single conflict but we all negotiate our way through life as well as in our parenting, whether we realise it or not. So, the question is not 'Should I negotiate?' but **'When and how?'** Keep in mind that some issues are not negotiable, things like keeping safe, being healthy, crossing the road sensibly, not playing with scissors, etc., so don't expend all your energy on negotiating the non-negotiable.

To sum up:

1. Face the problem.
2. Say how you feel and why.
3. Say what you would like to happen.
4. Stick to your guns but keep calm.
5. Negotiate if you have to – which means finding some common ground to leave room for compromise.
6. Monitor everyone's progress over time.

Communication

I dealt with the importance of communicating with children in Chapter 3, but I think the ultimate secret to communicating well with your kids is to remember to respect what they say and learn to listen to them properly – give them a chance to explain how they feel and give them your undivided attention. I always feel that words can build walls but they can also build bridges so choose your words carefully. At every age, children need you to understand how they're feeling. It's your job to make your child feel that they can talk to you about anything going on in their life and you achieve this by listening properly and not leaping in with your own judgements or constantly blaming them.

In many ways, it's much easier to communicate once your child has reached adolescence, as their understanding has greatly increased and they can be surprisingly sophisticated in their thinking. But you may find that it's also becoming impossible to use the controlling methods that may have worked when they were younger – so effective communication is essential to gain your older kids' co-operation.

Setting up good communication when your children are young gives you a head start for the teen years, when it will become even harder and the topics even more tricky and complicated. Unless you use the pre-teen years to openly discuss the moral issues of sex, drugs, and so on, the teen years are likely to be an endless power struggle.

Some Statements to Avoid

- **Sweeping generalisations.**

  We can all fall into this trap when we are tired, but making sweeping generalisations is something to avoid as it really doesn't help resolve a problem. When something happens that you don't like, don't blow it out of proportion by making across-the-board generalisations, and avoid starting sentences with **'You always…'** and **'You never…'**, as in: 'You always leave your toys out for me to trip over!' or 'You never do what I want you to do!' Stop and think about whether or not this is really true. Also, don't bring up past conflicts and wrongdoings as it merely stirs up more negativity and can damage your child's self-esteem as well as keeping you stuck rather than moving forward to what you do want to happen.

- **Being right.**

  It's damaging to decide that there's a 'right' and a 'wrong' way to look at things, and that your way of seeing things is right. Don't demand that your kids have to see things exactly the same way as you do, and don't take it as a personal attack if they have a different opinion. Always strive for a compromise or even a way to agree to disagree, and remember that there's not always a 'right' or a 'wrong', and that two points of view can both be valid.

Handling conflict is one of life's important lessons and rather than teaching your children to bottle things up and then explode it's helpful to teach them how to negotiate, talk openly and see problems and challenges from both sides so that they can learn to resolve issues at home before going out into the world. If you embrace this and teach your children about dealing with conflict and anger, you'll be more relaxed, confident and positive, which will benefit everyone in the long term.

6

Ways to Develop Your Child's Self-esteem

'There are only two lasting bequests we can give our children. One is roots, the other wings.' – Hodding Carter

When my dad died a couple of years ago, I remember looking back over our lives together and reflecting on what I truly loved and respected about him. I realised that the most precious gifts he had given me as a legacy were self-confidence and self-belief. In recent years the words 'self-confidence', 'self-esteem' and 'self-belief' seem to have become very fashionable 'buzz' words and they mean different things to different people. As I mentioned in Chapter 2, self-esteem is how you rate yourself deep down. It is a belief and a confidence in your own ability and value. It is not the same as arrogance and superiority, but a gentle knowledge that:

- You like yourself
- You think you're a good human being
- You deserve love
- You deserve happiness
- You feel deep down in your inner being that you are an okay person

As parents, we are forever being told about how we must nurture and not harm our child's self-esteem but how do we go about doing it? I believe self-esteem initially comes from you – as your child's parent you are the first role model your child has and you play a major part in developing, nurturing and building your child's confidence, their self-esteem and – in the long term – their self-belief.

So the first place to look is at yourself and to notice how you view the world – how confident and positive you feel inside, because you will unconsciously be passing that mindset and attitude on to your child. Develop your own confidence and positive mindset first as what you do and say, and how you act, really matters (see Chapter 2).

Did you know that on average we have 90,000 thoughts a day and that 60,000 of those are repetitive? So teach your child to think positively about themselves, and this will have a big impact on their happiness, attitude to life and success!

Awareness Parenting

A useful attitude to adopt as a parent is what I like to call 'awareness parenting'. By this I mean being constantly aware of the bigger picture. I think a great question to ask yourself in any situation is: 'Is this bringing me closer to or further away from the relationship I want with my child?' This will keep you firmly aware of the longer-term view and the need to be always building your child's inner confidence and self-esteem.

Help your child feel special and appreciated

One of the main factors that contributes to your child becoming resilient and confident is whether you focus your energy on your child's strengths and aren't constantly picking up on their weaknesses. Make a point to highlight lots of positive things. Become aware of when they get things right and praise them, smile at them or hug them – it all boosts positive self-belief and nurtures their soul.

High self-esteem is associated with solid problem-solving skills so encourage your child to 'struggle' with their laces for a little bit longer, with doing up their coat buttons or trying to manipulate something. Teach them to stick at completing their homework, or to keep at a task until they have finished it properly, as this builds up persistence and tenacity and your kids will learn the importance of finishing, which is a key skill to success in any endeavour in life. The feeling of having completed something gives kids a wonderful sense of achievement and is a great way for them to build their own inner self-confidence. Avoid comments that are judgemental; instead, frame them in more positive terms.

Provide choices for your child

I'm a great believer in providing what I call 'limited choices' to children, because providing small choices between two things really helps your child develop a sense of control over their life and builds their self-confidence. It also minimises those dreaded power struggles and tantrums. For example, ask your child if they would like to wear their green jumper or their blue jumper today – you still maintain control by making sure they are wearing a jumper as it's cold outside, but they feel they have made the choice and feel grown-up; this helps to set the foundations of them feeling in control of their lives. Or simply ask your child, 'Would you like to do your homework before or after dinner?' It appears to them that they are being given a choice, when in reality you are implying and still controlling the fact that they must do their homework!

Have fun playing around with offering limited choices as it builds independence and autonomy as well as nurturing your child's self-esteem.

Praise your child specifically

You need to instil in your children a strong, healthy self-image, because this will help everything else in life to become easier and more straightforward for them. By showing respect for your child – whether it's through listening to them properly, allowing them to make some limited choices about their lives, or by having confidence in them to solve a problem for themselves, you are building a foundation of self-confidence, self-worth and self-esteem. The next skill to develop is the ability to praise your child **positively**, **specifically and descriptively** as it is a fantastic tool in your communication toolkit for improving your parenting overall.

Be specific. Often parents mean well but praise with generalities such as… 'That's excellent', 'That's lovely', 'That's beautiful', and children really don't understand that type of praise as it's not specific enough.

Praise is more effective when divided into three parts:

1. Describe what you see in detail.

For example: 'In your drawing I see a big forest with green trees and yellow birds and lots of flowers. It makes me remember being in the countryside when we all had a great time camping. It makes me feel excited.'

This description gets down to the important details of what you are praising and helps children understand what you are valuing.

Here's an example that I used with my extremely untidy 17-year-old daughter!

'I see a really tidy room that's lovely to step into without any of your clothes on the floor, a tidy desk with all your perfumes and make-up in your make-up bag, I love it when you've made your bed with the duvet pulled up and the pillow at the top and your clothes all hung up in the wardrobe and you've pulled your curtains. Brilliant!'

After hearing such a wonderfully elaborate description, your child will then be able to praise him or herself and feel good about themselves.

2. Describe what you feel.

'It's really nice to be able to walk in here and feel relaxed as it looks like a super room and I'd like to spend time in here with you having a chat.'

This opens up a positive line of communication and helps build rapport and understanding between you.

3. Sum it all up in a simple word.

'Now that's what I call **organisation**!'

This is called descriptive praise and is a very powerful tool and useful skill to build up your child's self-esteem, regardless of their age. Try it now!

Highlight your child's strengths

One of my very popular techniques that I use with both parents and children is writing a 'Success Diary'. The Success Diary is a wonderful way to celebrate all the positive things your children have overcome, achieved or tried so far in their lives, and it focuses on their sense of personal success and personal achievements. It's rather like a giant pat on the back!

The Success Diary helps your children to focus on all the things that they can now do, or all the things – little or big – that they have achieved or overcome. It can be from learning to ride a bike, learning to swim, or picking up a certificate in judo, to coming through an illness or their parents' divorce. It can be from being a great friend, to passing their exams – the list is endless and also totally personal as success and achievement varies from person to person and one person's success is not someone else's.

Children need to celebrate what they get right, what they do well and what they have achieved so far, regardless of their age, as it builds self-esteem and confidence as well as motivation. It helps to keep your child moving forward positively and allows them to hold big dreams and high expectations for their lives.

So why not have some fun sitting down with your children with a piece of quality paper and getting them to draw a magnificent border full of colour and positive energy? Put on some fun and lively music to get you all in a really upbeat, positive state, and enjoy writing out and celebrating all the small and big successes of your child's life. You may discover that your child finds it difficult at first, as we have all been rather programmed to focus on what we get wrong rather than on what we get right, but stick with it and persevere as the smile at the end is worth its weight in gold, and your child's self-esteem is being nurtured, treasured and cherished. What a gift.

Have expanding high expectations and goals for your child

I work with many parents who struggle to hold high expectations for their children, but I also work with many who the media like to call 'pushy parents', who hold extremely high expectations for their offspring. I think it's helpful to strike some balance between the two.

Parents who have low self-esteem hold low expectations for their own lives and they consciously, and unconsciously, pass on those limiting beliefs and expectations to their children in the way they talk, how they act and what they do, because parents are their child's primary role models. Parents who hold uncomfortably high expectations for their children are also passing on their own issues around self-esteem and success to their children. So I am passionate about helping children find their own path, and their own way, by building on to their belief that they can achieve ANYTHING they set their mind to if they develop tenacity, determination and self-discipline.

I don't mind whether kids want to run their own business, be a plumber, dentist or work in McDonald's; I just want them to be clear about what they want to achieve in life. It's not all about owning fancy cars and being a footballer or winning *The X Factor*. It's about setting clear, long-term goals and teaching kids to walk towards them one small step at a time – weekly, monthly and yearly.

When I was a deputy head I worked with a lovely 11-year-old who was being bullied as she was really good at badminton and wanted to be in the 2016 Olympic team. We worked on her Success Diary and she wrote to me years later to say that she was well on her way to achieving her dream and her goal. How exciting and fabulous, and your child can be the same – able to manifest their dreams with the right encouragement, tenacity, support and positivity.

The Success Diary builds the mindset, attitude and determination for children to succeed in whatever they set their mind to. It's not about *my* definition of success or *yours* – it's about empowering children with the belief, skills and clarity they need to define what they want to get from life and want they want to give and contribute to life.

As parents, you need to teach your children that everyone experiences disappointments, setbacks and failures but it's how we teach our children to handle them that determines their success in life. Children need to learn from their setbacks and bounce back. **You** can teach them that mindset and how they deal with failure so that it doesn't stop them from trying again and again. Your attitude, mindset and the way you handle your life will have a direct impact on theirs so make sure you are modelling the attitude you want to pass on to them.

It's also important that you don't dash your child's dreams with 'Well that is NEVER going to happen, is it?' Don't limit or put a ceiling on what you think your child can achieve as that creates a limiting belief within them, and they will feel that they can't ever achieve something above your expectations of them.

Have fun exploring your child's unlimited potential.

Treat Your Child with Respect

Your relationship with your child is the foundation of their relationship with others. If you treat your child with compassion, kindness and respect, they will grow up to be concerned about others, caring, considerate and respectful towards others too, and most importantly they will learn to love and respect themselves – the key cornerstone in self-esteem, self-belief and self-confidence.

Just for this week, ponder the ways that you show your child respect:

- How do you speak to them?
- What tone of voice do you mostly use?
- What is your body language like most of the time?
- What messages are they getting from that?

Children are accustomed to their parents communicating with a lot of ordering, correcting and directing, so by exploring my techniques not only will these strategies demonstrate your respect for your children, but each suggestion goes a long way in fostering your child's autonomy and capability too.

Giving Children Positive Feedback

> *'Children need love, especially when they do not deserve it.'*
> ~ Harold Hulbert

Children respond to the world according to their perception and experience of it, and very often it's not the same as your perception of the world. This is where arguments, rows and conflicts begin, when their map of the world doesn't fit in with yours. Yet a child's map of the world can sometimes catch you by surprise and make you think again.

When teaching and guiding children, it is really helpful to step into their shoes and socks for a minute or two and see the world from their eyes, hear the world from their ears and feel how the situation feels to them, as it shifts your perception of the event or situation and helps you be more tolerant and understanding.

No matter how honourable your intentions are for your kids, it is how the message is received by a child that counts. What you say, and how you say it, influences how well you are understood. It also affects how others respond to you. So it is helpful to think about the words you use, your tone of voice, body language and the vibes you're giving out (I've covered this in more detail in Chapter 3).

Your positive parenting checklist

- Children pick up more from what you don't say than what you do, so be mindful of your attitude and mood.
- Have the end in mind and know what you actually want to achieve by disciplining, guiding or teaching them.
- Have the child's best interests at heart before you talk with them, and respect their age and maturity.
- Be in a positive, relaxed, centred place yourself before talking or chastising them as this takes the emotional charge out of the whole thing and keeps you firmly in control.
- Ask yourself, 'Is this moving me further towards the long-term relationship I want to build with my child or is it moving me further away?' 'How am I making my child feel cherished and loved, especially now when they're misbehaving?'
- Remember to share feelings rather than blame and say things like, 'When you…I feel…because…' This shifts the atmosphere into being more specific through positively stating what you do want to see more of and expressing how you feel about what's happened.
- Try to put forward suggestions rather than always giving commands. Just be mindful of your tone of voice and never plead, as this gives away your power. Speak confidently and 'mean business'. Remember that what you say is non-negotiable.
- Think about the timing of when you want to give kids feedback and ask yourself when it is a good time to raise a topic – maybe after the immediate issue is over, and not at stressful times. Strike when the iron is cold!
- Hold back from hurtful words, name-calling or negative references, bringing up the past or making comparisons to other children as it diminishes the child's self-esteem.
- And finally ask yourself, 'What can this child learn from this experience?' And get the child, no matter how old they are, to

ask themselves, 'What did I learn from this?' as this will be a far more empowering experience and useful lifetime habit to get into.

We all make mistakes and parenthood is all about learning to be patient. The most important thing in life is to help children learn from their mistakes so that they can take the valuable lessons they need and don't keep on making the same mistakes over and over again. Help your children to see feedback as something positive, moving them forward with fine-tuning their life, not as criticism, which is disempowering, judgemental and negative and will forever hold them back. Teach them to pick themselves up, dust themselves off and have another go.

The Importance of A Positive Self-image

Self-belief is like a muscle – if you use it regularly it will get stronger and grow. With regular exercise you will be able to cope with whatever life throws at you. By the same principle, if you fail to regularly exercise this muscle, it becomes limp, weak and flabby. When you rely wholly on yourself and build up your self-reliance, you experience a quality that only truly powerful individuals share: the belief in your own ability to make good things happen.

Self-reliance is the key that will open up a world of fearlessness, freedom and opportunity. When you believe in your own strengths you can achieve great things and have a determination not to quit. Only then will you experience what separates high achievers from their critics. The powerful person is within. It is my passion to help you as a parent give this wonderful gift to your children, like a ripple in a pond, each generation building on the last. In every situation in life, whether it's business, relationships or romance, neediness and displays of insecurity make people feel uncomfortable. As the relationship expert Chuck Spezzano says: 'When you're needy, you're hungry and the other person feels they're your lunch!'

Children need to be given a strong, healthy self-image, because from that solid foundation, everything else in life will become easier and more straightforward for them. The first book I ever wrote was called *Music for the Soul – How to Give Your Kids the Gift of Self Esteem* and it was inspired by my own father and mother who gave me that wonderful gift.

Your current self-image is the result of the repeated messages and instructions you received as a child from your authority figures. The way you see yourself today is the result of conditioning by your parents, family, teachers and other influential adults and peers in your life.

The way you think about yourself determines everything you do, say, act and believe because the world around you is a reflection of your inner world. Whatever you see outside, you have a parallel inside. The inner world is the one that gives you the feeling and belief that you are okay. The outer world enables you to appear and behave in a manner that looks like you are self-assured. Both the inner and outer types of confidence support each other.

So it's very important to give your children the gift of inner and outer confidence. I have written all about this in Chapter 2.

Simple Ways to Improve Your Child's Self-esteem

Bedtime is an excellent opportunity to chat with your children about their day and to improve their self-esteem. Develop a simple but regular habit that before your children go off to sleep you find time to talk about the day together and let them know what you are proud of them for, what they have got **right** that day and that you notice all these wonderful things about them. Share with them just how special they are. Develop the habit of telling your children positive things to nurture their self-esteem as they fall asleep. They will have lovely dreams and wake up positive, upbeat and ready to embrace the next day positively. Say things like, 'I noticed today that you were easily on time.' 'I noticed how thoughtful you were.' 'I saw you really thinking about how to solve that problem with your homework tonight – well done for sticking at it.' 'I noticed how organised you were.' 'I noticed how patient you were with your sister.'

I am special because…

At my confidence workshops for children, I build each child's confidence by asking them to sit in a circle and putting a Magic Chair in the centre of the circle where the child whose turn it is sits. We all then have to look the child in the eyes (as your eyes are the windows to your soul according to an English proverb) and give the child the gift of being told why they are special. Each child says the same phrase starting with 'You Are Special Because…' They follow this with things such as: you are a good friend to me, a great dancer, runner, swimmer, footballer. You are great at maths, jigsaws, drawing, being helpful, organising games, writing stories, painting, being patient, you are resilient, resourceful, funny.

This is a magical thing to do as the child learns to receive a whole host of sincere compliments and to see how appreciated they are for all their unique and special gifts and talents. I always find it makes me feel very emotional as the children come up with lovely and individual things to say and I write them down and at the end of the workshop give the child a scroll with what everyone has said, wrapped up with a red ribbon. The children keep these scrolls and I encourage them to look at their 'I Am Special' list when they are feeling sad, upset or are having a tough time as it lifts their spirits and reminds them of just how loved and special they are.

I have had letters back eight years later thanking me for the gift I gave the child that day as they still have that scroll hidden away in their bedroom.

It's a very simple idea that you could do at home around your kitchen table and you could all enjoy receiving the gift of knowing why you are special.

Wall of fame

Every child is good at something. Discover it, encourage it, frame it and display it. If your home is missing a Wall of Fame your child is missing their moment of fame and the opportunity to celebrate their successes. Consider all the things you could recognise, celebrate and commemorate with your children to build their self-esteem and their self-confidence, from becoming a pen writer, swimming a length, being Player Of The Year to getting their orange judo belt. All the wonderfully diverse unique and special successes that each of your children achieves. You will be giving them the gift of self-esteem and the smile on their face will say it all.

Try activities and hobbies that they enjoy, as this will naturally and easily develop their self-esteem. With Boy Scouts and Girl Guides everyone wins and they get lots of badges. As children walk past their Wall of Fame, they can see at a glance five to ten years' worth of achievement. This gives them a lift, especially during times when their self-worth is faltering.

The Easy Button Technique

Imagine if you had a button in your kitchen that your kids could run over and press any time they did something new, overcame something difficult, did something they found unpleasant or out of their comfort zone, or just had a go!

I first used this technique during a confidence workshop for kids, using a fun button that says, 'That was EASY!', which I bought from a stationery shop. It's a really simple and brilliant way to anchor confidence in a child's unconscious and to attach doing new things and having a go to feelings of success, as it builds confidence and self-esteem instantly through just having fun and being relaxed. Kids run over and push their 'That was EASY!' button and laugh!

An anchor is when your mood changes in response to some trigger or stimulus and your unconscious registers it every time you see, hear or feel it. A bit like going to the fridge to get a snack after seeing an advert on the TV, or like jumping up at a party when your favourite song comes on that reminds you of going to college, someone's birthday or a romance in which it's become 'our song'!

Building and anchoring confidence with a 'That was EASY!' button is a funny and wonderfully positive experience for kids. Kids love it and use it all the time and I have had inventive and funny stories sent to me from parents all over the world who love using it too. Think of the power to their confidence after they've learnt their seven times table, how to tie their shoelaces or use the potty, done their homework, answered the phone and taken a message, practised the piano, tidied their room, put away their toys, read their reading book, and then ran over and pressed the 'That was EASY!' button! The list is endless and only limited by your imagination.

What a simple way to boost your child's self-esteem and develop the 'have a go' mentality so important to success in life. Just imagine if families started to do this fun thing from the moment their kids were born...think how much more relaxed, optimistic and happy kids would be.

You could use it, too, at times when you didn't shout, didn't nag or got something right with your kids or when you did something new for the first time, like struggling with the frustration over online banking, speaking up at a meeting or salsa dancing.

I am passionate about helping kids grow up free from the crippling effects of low self-esteem and this is a really easy, inexpensive and fun idea. Pass it on to all your friends and let's make growing up positive! Get one for your kitchen, office, classroom or nursery...and your whole family can have fun making life, learning and living more rewarding.

Wouldn't it be wonderful if all nurseries, schools, colleges, gymnastics clubs, dance clubs and sports clubs had a 'That was EASY!' button, too?

Positive Tips for Developing Self-esteem Through the Ages and Stages

Toddlers

Toddlers, unlike newborns, are obsessed with learning and increasingly look to explore their world, touching and tasting everything. You can help build confidence by making your child's world a safe place to explore. Set limits, but don't be too quick to say, 'Don't touch that!'

- Be a safe home base for your toddler. When your toddler goes off to explore, be there when they get stuck or require encouragement. Children who trust their parents feel safe and learn to go out and explore the world.
- When talking to your toddler allow them sufficient time to finish what they are trying to say.
- Praise your child's successes: picture the joy on your child's face when they push the correct button or place a block through the right hole. Imagine that smile getting even bigger when you notice and tell them what a good job they did figuring out the problem.
- Be patient with them and try not to show impatient body language, such as sighing or foot-tapping.
- Answer any questions using simple language that they can understand.
- Spend some time each day doing nothing else but talking exclusively with your toddler.
- Let them help you. They can probably bring you things that you've asked for or help put things back into their toy box. Show them just how proud you are of them.
- Give your toddler opportunities to succeed in new situations and help your little one take small steps in the direction of achievement and accomplishment. Freely use the phrases, 'I'll do it with you,' and say things like, 'I know it's a bit tricky to do that, but I'll be with you. Let's just give it a try shall we?'
- Resist comparisons. Comments such as 'Why can't you be more like your sister?', even if you say it in jest, will damage your child's self-esteem and their confidence and will just foster shame, envy and competition. So let your child know you appreciate them for being their unique, special and individual self and you will build long-term confidence.

Nursery and pre-school

Children this age love to act like little adults. They like to do things they see their parents and older brothers and sisters doing. So take the time to teach your child new things. They are eager to learn and want to please you. A pre-schooler learns a lot by doing; for example, they get satisfaction out of drawing a picture, but may not really care how it turns out.

Help your child prepare for school by:

- Encouraging your children to play with other children and allow opportunities for them to be with adults who are not family members.
- Having a positive attitude towards school.
- Talking to your child and explaining that it's okay to be scared and that everybody else will be feeling the same way. Explain that you will be there when they get home and will help them with any problem they have no matter how small.

School-aged children 5–11

With school-aged children, you won't have as many opportunities for conversation as you did with your younger child as they will be at school all day, and as your child grows up, they may turn to you less frequently, so you may need to make a special effort to spend time together and **find time to talk**.

Here are some practical ideas to keep the conversation going and to build your child's self-esteem:

- **Speak to your school-aged child in a mature fashion.**
  School-aged children want their 'bigness' and maturity acknowledged. They may be offended if they feel they are

being spoken to like a toddler (even if they happen to be acting like one). So be mindful of the way you approach topics like tidying their room or doing their homework and offer them limited choices, as discussed in Chapter 6, which are a brilliant way to give autonomy and self-esteem to your maturing child while still being in charge. Speaking in this way appeals to your child's 'bigness' and is much more successful than just nagging and saying 'How many times do I have to tell you to do your homework!'

- **Ask your school-aged child specific, rather than general, questions.**
  Instead of asking a question such as, 'How was school?', which most children seem to close down to, try more open-ended questions like, 'Did your teacher read your great story that you wrote over the weekend yet?' Also avoid leading questions like, 'Do you think that's an appropriate way to speak to me?' as they often backfire and can lead to more confrontation. Instead, you might say, 'I feel angry when you talk to me that way. I would like you to think about your tone of voice next time.'

  Listen to your school-aged child without contradicting them. Instead of saying, 'That's ridiculous', you might simply say, 'Hmm', or 'Really?' Then, ask specific questions based on the situation your child has described as this also shows them you are truly listening, are interested in what they have to say and are taking them seriously, which will also build their self-esteem.

- **Repeat what you heard your child say, but in a more mature way.**
  You can reflect their statement in the form of a question, implying, 'Am I getting this right?' In this way, you are respecting

your child's intelligence, making them feel understood and encouraging them to tell you more. You might say, 'So, you think your class teacher is stupid, but you don't want me to go to the school and get involved? Can you tell me what you are upset about?'

- **Laugh a little and admit your mistakes.**
  At times, humour is the best way to resolve a dispute, react to an upset or make a request of your school-aged child. You can also ask your child for help in figuring out what to do. Kids love to hear parents admit they were wrong. You might say, 'Am I making a mess of this? Should we try to figure it out in a different way? What do you think?'

- **Ask your child to help set their own limits.**
  Don't be afraid to say 'No' when your school-aged child needs it. However, within reason, your child can make some rules too at this age, which builds up a great relationship between you. For instance, you might ask them to propose a sensible and reasonable time for them to begin their homework. Discuss it and then back off. Ask your child to be the boss of deciding what help is given, how much and when (in accordance with their teacher's instructions) because in this way, you are helping your child to feel in control of their world.

- **Keep talking even if your school-aged child won't talk to you.**
  You may feel at times that you have lost your credibility with your school-aged child if you take their silence or impulsive remarks personally, and your relationship can suffer if you do. Just relax and celebrate that your child is growing up and maturing and is simply trying to establish their independence, which is a healthy sign.

Older kids 12–18

- **Follow their lead.**

  Each child has their own way of reaching out to you and your willingness to take the invitation will carry you both a long way, building the long-term relationship you really want with your older children. While it's easy to overlook your daughter's constant invitations to 'come here and see this!' as an annoying interruption, the truth is, she is including you in her interests and world. By saying yes as often as you can, you are meeting her where she's happy to join you and the relationship will develop easily and naturally by you following her lead. My own daughter invites me to help her plan her outfits for going out with her friends – not because she can't decide but because she wants to connect with me so I follow her lead and we chat, have fun and she always ultimately decides (unless the skirt's too short!)

- **Stay on the lookout for new openings.**

  New interests and hobbies provide new opportunities for you both to connect and discuss what's going on from a slightly different perspective. One of the most fascinating things about watching children grow up is realising that each new development challenge always carries with it a new opportunity to reconnect. From always reading to your younger child perhaps you could enjoy listening to their stories or essays as they read them out loud to you and you just swap over your role.

- **Take charge**.

  Kids aren't responsible for staying close to you; it's your job to remain a constant available resource to them. If you're struggling to make a meaningful connection, take the initiative to create the environment where something can happen. Long car rides, new outings, asking for input, going out for a pizza, inviting your kids to teach you some ways to master all the ever-changing technology; all these things can really open doors for easy, relaxed conversations that can take you somewhere fun and new as a family.

- **Don't apologise for your desire to stay connected.**
  All kids go through phases where they want to assert their independence and pull back a little. Don't let this fool you into thinking that they need you any less. By continuing to state your desire to be with them, spend time together and hear their thoughts, you keep the door open for them to talk with you whenever the time feels right, in an easy, relaxed and loving way.

- **Be affectionate.**
  The hugs and cuddles may change into high fives and pats on the back or a friendly squeeze of their arm, but there's a lot of security for your emerging teenager in knowing that you will reach out – even when they are moody and uncommunicative – to show them just how much you still love them, no matter what.

Express Your Love and Affection

All that children want, need and deserve is unconditional love. Children and adults thrive on affection, emotional attachment, love and devotion. Children have a great need to love and be loved. They also need to know that they belong and will always have a place in their families no matter what.

You show your child you care by getting along with them, respecting them, hugging and smiling at them, laughing and joking, and showing your joy and pleasure with them. Your children will imitate what you do and what you are, not what you want them to be. Children learn love from parents – love for themselves and love for others.

Self-esteem begins with receiving unconditional love and support and letting your child know that they are normal, but also different and unique. Remember that you can rob and erode self-esteem by ridicule, humiliation and, of course, by hitting them.

Children from affectionate families are better equipped to cope with the frustrations and disappointments of daily life. They develop self-esteem, self-worth, self-confidence and ultimately self-belief from being unconditionally loved. This doesn't mean you become lenient with them or lower your expectations, or just give them material possessions. Children need and thrive on their safe limits.

You can never give too much genuine affection, warmth or love to your child. Don't think your child will become spoiled by all the attention. Holding back and being aloof just sends out the wrong message. Children don't need the old-school way of toughening up. They are fragile, sensitive, small human beings who need hugs, fun and laughter, just as much from their fathers as from their mothers.

Children who are truly loved have a strong sense of security and are less needy. The healthiest adults are the ones who express their love to others easily because they grew up with unequivocal and unconditional love from their parents. Those who were forced to scrape by on less than complete affection are the needy adults.

Be physical

Children need plenty of physical affection, not just when they are little, but throughout their childhood. We are tactile creatures and need physical contact with others. The rise of aromatherapy and all sorts of massages, reflexology, Indian head massage, etc., are symbolic of our need to be touched. Touching stimulates growth, reduces stress and helps the immune system to work better.

We need to remember that the real foundation of a parent/child relationship is emotional and physical, as well as intellectual. The way you express your love, however, may change as your child develops. I remember my own son squirming as I gave him a big, noisy hug and kiss goodbye at the school gate in front of his friends. He was so embarrassed, possibly because I was also a teacher at his school! I had forgotten that at 12 he'd rather I hugged him at home and played it cool at school. I needed to learn sensitivity to his changing needs. Teenagers still need displays of affection too, of course, but remember to keep this part of your relationship more private during this stage of their development.

Praise your child

Praising children is another way to express your love for them. It not only makes them feel good about themselves, therefore building their self-esteem, but it also helps them to learn important lessons about the value of working hard to achieve a goal or to behave in a certain way. It is worth thinking about how you phrase your praise. Try to be specific rather than to link the accomplishment to your affection. Genuinely praise the leaflet your son has designed, looking at the attention to detail and the content; not just saying, 'I love it when you work hard at school.' Then there is no judgement or pressure put on your child, just a willingness to praise the positive.

Praise your child's accomplishment for the effort and energy put into it, rather than relying on the natural talent. We rewarded our son with a trip to see Chelsea play in Barcelona, before we knew his exam results, to reward his time, energy and commitment to studying for weeks beforehand, and going the extra mile to get into his secondary school. Our daughter felt our heartfelt praise and delight at her singing festival, because she had to overcome her shyness at performing in public, not because she received a certificate. Look at sporting stars like Frank Lampard, Jonny Wilkinson or Sir Steve Redgrave. They are successful because they work harder and practise more than their peers, regardless of how naturally talented they are. They are determined to put in time, energy and commitment. Give this determination to your child and watch them soar with enthusiasm and self-esteem.

Link your praise to the quality of the accomplishment, not just to the grade or value someone else puts on it. Children are painfully aware, by around the age of nine years old, that their accomplishments are being graded and evaluated by others. Praise the improved spelling, not the 76 per cent mark. Compare, if you must, your child's performance or level of accomplishment to themselves, not to others. For example, say, 'You can really control the netball and can really throw it accurately to another player now. Well done, that's brilliant!' rather than, 'You always play better than Zoe. I don't know why she is on the team.' Competition is tough enough without you adding your parental expectations and living your life through your child.

Beware, however, of false praise. Don't pretend. Children can see through you, very easily, and don't deserve to be patronised. Focus on how they might do better next time.

Be careful what you say

Being a parent, and particularly a single parent, is emotionally, physically, mentally and spiritually demanding as you are setting limits, sharing wisdom, cooking dinner, looking for lost football boots and old geography textbooks, offering advice, being a role model and needing to be an adult in your own right too. It is draining, and sometimes it is just tough to figure out what exactly your child's needs are at the moment. If she is three and crying, and it's 9pm, then she is just plain tired. But if, at the age of thirteen, your child suddenly just loses it over something trivial, it can be very demanding.

The important response to be aware of is the 'auto parent' or the one you hear yourself revert to when you're tired or stressed, that sounds just like your mother! The one that says, 'If you don't brush your teeth, Molly, you'll end up with black teeth and no boyfriends!' Ouch! This is reacting, under stress, to how you were reared and may not be the parent you truly want to be.

If you have unresolved issues from your childhood, it's a good idea to have a close look at them and be aware of them, so that you can have more control over your patterns of behaviour.

To sum up:

- Give your child love, attention and affection.
- Spend time alone with them.
- Take interest in their hobbies and opinions.
- Be a good listener.
- Give your child chances to try new things, especially if they show an interest or talent in something, such as painting.
- Give your child specific praise. Instead of just saying, 'You did a great job,' put an arm around your child and say, 'You were very responsible today. You came home and did your homework without any reminders. I could tell you were working hard. Well done you.'
- Set a good example. Show that your own self-esteem is important. Instead of complaining about, for example, your weight, say, 'I feel great when I exercise. I'm going to take a jog after

dinner.' Make sure you speak in positive ways to inspire and teach them to feel good about themselves.

- Praise your child for their effort, e.g. 'I know you're sad that you didn't make the football/netball team, but I'm proud of you for trying. It took a lot of courage and hard work!'

I think nurturing your child's self-esteem is the biggest gift you can give them, coupled with unconditional love, because from these solid foundations a child can grow up free from the crippling effects of low self-esteem and low self-worth, able to flourish and blossom to enjoy a full and varied life.

7

Balancing Your Personal, Family and Work Time

'*Imagine life as a game in which you are juggling five balls in the air. You name them – work, family, health, friends, and spirit – and you're keeping all of these in the air. You will soon understand that work is a rubber ball. If you drop it, it will bounce back. But the other four balls – family, health, friends, and spirit are made of glass. If you drop one of these, they will be irrevocably scuffed, marked, nicked, damaged, or even shattered. They will never be the same. You must understand that and strive for balance in your life.*' – Brian Dyson, CEO of Coca-Cola Enterprises

Managing Your Time

Are you stuck in the spin cycle of life…exhausted, wrung out and dizzy? Do you find yourself falling into bed worn out, frustrated and complaining, 'Where did the time GO?' Then welcome to the club! You are not alone; I coach lots of manic mums and dazed dads who are crying out for help and desperate to get all the jobs done, have some quality time with the kids, and each other, and have some fun and laughter along the way too.

When you have kids, your life changes and so does your whole concept of time. Everything seems to take longer...as kids walk slower, talk slower, think slower and eat slower than you do, and they don't seem to worry about rushing or have any sense of time, whether they are toddlers or teens. Maybe, just maybe, there's a lesson in there somewhere.

It's a busy, frenetic and hectic world and often having fun, relaxing and chilling out slip down our list of priorities and get left on the shelf because kids are demanding of your time whatever their age. So, what can you do about it? Well, I think it helps if you see time as your friend and your most precious commodity. Think about the words and phrases you use to describe time as this will reveal your attitude and mindset to managing your time. Do you say you spend time, lose time, save time, kill time, waste time, let time slip away, take time for granted, squander time or can't find the time? Or do you say you use time, spend time wisely, value time, organise your time, treasure time, schedule or plan time, or make time?

It's all about the way you view it, and parents with a sense of more balance in their life find time, make time and plan time with their kids. The secret is balance and recognising that time is your most valuable resource when you have kids, regardless of their ages, and we all have 24 hours in a day so it's about how you prioritise your time and how you ring-fence it.

The key thing is to make good choices and develop good habits with time. A successful life is really no more than a string of successful days – so why not start today to become more successful in managing your time? Let's look at some simple steps to help you along the way.

Keep it simple, stupid

There are loads of wonderful books and workshops out there to teach you about mastering your time, but I think it helps to KISS or 'Keep It Simple and Straightforward'.

Architects and builders have drawing plans; pilots have flight plans. Business executives have business plans; coaches have game plans; and teachers have lesson plans. So why don't parents have 'parenting plans'?

Some people call it a 'to do' list or a list of priorities for the day, some life coaches call it 'daily goal setting', which all sounds a bit pretentious and hard going to me, so call it what you like. Whatever you call it, get into the habit of doing it and build in time for your children and family. Of all the positive things you'll ever do, investing your time in your family and your kids – even if it's only 10 minutes a day – will pay off a thousand times in good-will, affection, love and appreciation from your children. The feelings of accomplishment will really astound you as you build this new habit in to your life and you'll watch your relationships easily, effortlessly and massively improve as they grow and flourish over time.

Another useful skill to develop is the ability to delegate, whether it's at work or at home. Sharing the load by assigning some of your tasks to another person helps them develop responsibility as well as helping to free up some of your valuable time to do more productive or more important tasks. So start to look at how you can find tasks to delegate to other people that they can do even better than you can – or you may need to spend a little extra time showing others who are less experienced but keen to learn how to do something that in the long term will give you back so much more useful, quality and valuable time. So spend time teaching your daughter how to mow the lawn or give the office junior a lesson in how to answer the phone correctly.

Learn to prioritise

We all juggle – with relationships, parenting, life and work – and sometimes we drop one, or all, of the balls! The first myth we need to debunk is that you can actually get the balance completely right. You can't. But I can help you focus on effective strategies that make you feel more in control and back in the driving seat of your life. How many times do you focus on the negative feelings and anxieties related to work and home and forget to focus on the positive things that happen in your life, with your kids or career? With a simple shift and a positive refocusing, changes can happen almost overnight in how you see your life. By simply reframing how you describe work, you can change your view of it.

I am very passionate and enthusiastic about my work and because I love it so much it doesn't feel like work but there is also a down side to that, in that I don't know when to stop, close the door and switch off, and I also expect everyone to feel the same about my work – which is just plain barmy of me really. But here's the reality. No matter how much we do, we will never get everything done. There isn't enough time for all the things that need doing, all of what we want to do, would like to do or think we should do. So it helps to relax and remember that we won't get it all done immediately and to let things roll over to the next day – we need to be more forgiving of ourselves.

Everyone is different when it comes to what the 'ideal balance' should feel like in their lives. The balance changes with time, circumstance and stage of life anyway. The really important thing is that you know what you mean and are very clear about what your priorities are in each area of your life. The secret is to remain flexible on life's journey and have a clear idea of your destination because that allows you to change direction if you want to stop off, smell the roses and take a detour.

Ask yourself regularly, at least three times a day:

- Am I being productive or just busy?
- Am I inventing things to do to avoid the important?

Some important things to bear in mind:

- Don't try too hard at the wrong things!
- Make the difficult leap of dissociating effort and reward.
- Learn to be intelligently lazy or productively lazy, which is another way of saying: work less; achieve more.
- And finally, practise the art of non-finishing. Starting something doesn't automatically mean that you have to finish it. Develop the ability to stop.

Time Takers

When I was a teacher I remember using a great big, bright-red egg timer on Friday afternoons during 'Golden Time' to give some time out to the naughty kids who couldn't behave themselves during the more relaxed half hour of free play and fun activities. They had to sit and watch the egg timer for two or three minutes while the other kids had fun and played around them.

It made me look at time in a different way. What if the egg timer was filled with rainbow-coloured magic fairy dust instead of sand...how would we all look at time then as it ran out? Would we see time as precious, magical, delightful and special? Would we use time more effectively and abundantly and carefully?

Just like eating a chocolate bar or sipping a deliciously hot, frothy latte, we always want more when we're finished, but with **time** you can't just reach inside your pocket and buy another one. When it's gone...it's gone. So it's not about how much time you've got, it's about how you choose to spend it.

Recognising that you actually have a choice is very empowering and can be life-changing for some parents I work with. Start to notice this week how you are spending your time because before you can save time you need to know how you use it. Time can drip away like the leaky tap in the bathroom if you're not careful.

- Start to notice how long you spend on the phone or texting every day. How much time do you waste that could be used more efficiently and effectively somewhere else? What would be the benefits to cutting that down?
- How much time do you spend watching TV? Could you make some changes there?
- How long do you spend chatting at the school playground, nursery or at work?
- Do you find yourself totally hijacked by e-mails every day? What if you only opened them at 12pm and 4pm so that you could then answer the most important ones? How much time would that free up?
- If you stopped worrying about things you can't control, how much more energy would you have?
- How much time do you spend clearing up after others? What if you asked for help, delegated some tasks and allowed your kids to become more independent and helpful?
- What if you stopped being a perfectionist and left the ironing for a couple of days and ignored the dust in the dining room?
- What are your personal 'time takers' and what can you do to change them this week?
- How would it feel if you took control of time and didn't let it take control of you?

Feeling in control of your life and getting a good work/home balance is about not letting time control you. It's about sitting down each night for just a few minutes and jotting down what you want to achieve the next day – it keeps you focused on the important things, keeps you moving steadily forward and stops you becoming overwhelmed. It also gives you clarity, direction and a sense of achievement, particularly if you tick the list off at the end of each day.

What would you do if I could wave a magic wand and you had an extra, 25th, hour? What would you do with it…more ironing, more paperwork? Or would you spend it laughing with your kids, and smelling the jasmine in the garden?

Take responsibility for managing your time this week and see the change that you can make to your stress levels by simply being in charge of your own time.

Eliminating Guilt

I've lost count of how many times I've worked with mums in particular on their overwhelming feelings of guilt – the 'BIG G' gremlin of parenting! Whether they are working mums, stay-at-home mums or part-time mums, women seem to be programmed to feel guilty and it just holds us all back, keeps us stuck and is really anger turned in on ourselves as we find it difficult to ask for help, delegate parenting jobs or share our needs with others. It's also caused by wanting to be a perfect parent.

I know first-hand all about the feelings of guilt. I remember when my mum was ill in hospital with emphysema a few years ago and no matter how many times I went all the way to the hospital during a week, it never seemed to be enough; and if I brought her prawn sandwiches she would want cheese, and if I brought cheese she would want prawn. I could never seem to please her and I felt enormously guilty about how much time I spent with her, how many times I went and how I never felt I did enough. I battled feeling guilty about leaving the kids to do their homework without me, rushing back to prepare my lessons for the next day as I was teaching at the time too. I felt torn and pulled in many directions and I felt guilty no matter how hard I tried to do what was 'right' for everyone.

So what is guilt?

Guilt is often a message from within that you have violated your own high standards, or from others trying to make you feel guilty as they may want to have a hold over you, even unconsciously. It can come from working parents feeling guilty about their work/life balance, from parents feeling guilty about losing their temper, not playing enough with their kids, not spending enough time with their partner or elderly mother, feeling guilty about being separated or divorced or about having to leave work at 5.00 instead of 5.30 to pick up their child from after-school care. The list is endless.

Guilty feelings can come from within, be handed down to you from parents, teachers or people of influence when you were young, from lack of self-esteem or from controlling partners or former partners. Guilty feelings can also be tied up with remorse, regret and feelings of responsibility for others or for situations that you find yourself in.

Guilt is also a feeling of struggling with what you 'should', 'ought' and 'must' do and feels like a battle between what you 'want to do', 'what you'd like to do' and 'what you'd like to choose to do'. The feelings of guilt, regret and remorse are among some of the strongest and most powerful emotions that we want to avoid as they are so painful. They keep us stuck, trapped and eddying around feeling like a victim because they are so negative. They can make you become over-responsible, striving to make life 'right' for everyone and can make you feel exhausted and overwhelmed. Guilt can make you resentful, frustrated and helpless and can lead to depression, drinking too much or having great anger or rage, none of which are healthy or beneficial to family life.

Nearly all parents I have worked with have experienced some form of guilt – whether it's a feeling that they haven't done enough for their children or a sense of guilt over choosing to do something for themselves without their kids. It's also sometimes due to not feeling worthy or deserving enough and can lead to being a martyr. Whatever brings up feelings of guilt for you, it leaves you disempowered and it often won't go away by itself. It just grows and gets stronger, and can mislead or misdirect you about moving forward in your life.

Often underneath the feelings of guilt are irrational, limiting beliefs that need to be shifted. Things like:

- I don't deserve to be happy.
- I am responsible for my family's (spouse's) happiness.
- There is only one 'right' way to do things.
- My children should never suffer in their childhood like I did in mine.
- My kids should have more material things than I did.
- It is my fault if others in my life are not happy.
- If my kids fail in any way, it's my responsibility.
- It is wrong to be concerned about myself.
- People are constantly judging and criticising me and what they think is important to me.
- No matter what I do, I am always wrong.

Some parents suppress guilt, some wallow in it and stay helpless and stuck, while others use it as a huge lever for positive change and this is what I want to help you with now. The key is to be able to acknowledge the feeling for what it is and to learn from it. When you let go of the guilt, you can actually be a better, more relaxed parent. To ease your guilt, focus on all the positive things that you bring to your family and write them down – this really helps you to see the enormous amount of things you get right and do well. Learn to accept that you are an individual with interests and passions beyond just your role as a parent and learn to forgive yourself because you are doing your best and doing a great job.

Top tips for overcoming guilt

- Acknowledge that you have it.
- Take control and don't keep going over and over it inside your head – let it go. Release guilt in the same way as you would anger (see Anger-management strategies in Chapter 5 for some ideas).
- Don't allow guilt to turn into feelings of inadequacy.
- Reflect on the role guilt is playing in your life at the moment by choosing a current problem and writing down the answers to the following questions:
  - What problem is currently troubling me?
  - Who is responsible for the problem?
  - Whose problem is it, really?
  - What have I done to make this problem worse for myself?
  - How much guilt do I feel about this problem on a scale of 1–10 (10 being the highest)?
  - How much does the guilt I experience exaggerate or exacerbate my problem?
  - If I felt no more guilt, what would my problem look like then?

Now relax and breathe deeply and slowly and imagine I have just waved a magic wand and made the feelings of guilt disappear. What do you see, hear and feel now?

Ask your unconscious what small change you need to make to feel more in control of your life this week. Ask yourself:

- Does this problem have more than one solution?
- Do I simply need to express my frustration and ask for support or a helping hand?
- Is it my problem or actually someone else's?
- Am I taking on another's responsibility and not allowing them to experience being independent?
- Am I trying to keep another from experiencing pain, hardship or discomfort?

If you discover that the problem is really someone else's, give it back to the person to solve and deal with. It's not your responsibility to solve the world's problems or to constantly rescue someone else from their problems. If you feel uncomfortable leaving the person 'stranded' with their issue, a simple way forward is to find practical ways to empower them, perhaps by suggesting some solutions or new ways of doing things. You need to become slightly detached and more efficient in handling stressful and challenging situations, rather than taking on someone else's 'stuff'.

Imagine that 'guilt' is an object that you can take out of your body and package up in a lovely box. Give it a colour, texture and feeling, and now imagine climbing to the highest mountain you can find and throwing it off a cliff. Do you feel lighter? Good – now every morning and evening, just before you brush your teeth, look in the mirror and say some positive affirmations to build your confidence and empower yourself. Say things like:

- I am grounded, centred, positive and happy with myself.
- I make good decisions for the highest good of everyone – including myself.
- I deserve to solve this problem positively.
- I deserve to be kind and forgiving of myself.
- I deserve to do my best and feel good about my decisions.
- I deserve to have other people be good to me, too!

If you learn to see guilt as a way to help you make changes in your life, then it has a positive intention. Guilt is there to allow you to learn from your mistakes and take control, and to help you keep up the standards and values that you have set for yourself in life. So master its message and move forward – not looking back in the rear-view mirror.

'Me' Time

'Me' time could be the best hours you give not only yourself but also your children. As a parent you are often the lynchpin of your whole family. If you are tired, stressed and snappy, chances are your whole family is tense, as they take their lead from you and pick up on your vibes. So, how do you get the balance right in being upbeat and enthusiastic rather than selfless and exhausted?

One of the first things I encourage parents to do is to remember what they enjoyed doing before they had kids, as this releases positive, happy memories and helps relax you. Was it sitting down with a cup of coffee and a magazine for half an hour, going to a film with your partner, having a bubble bath with your favourite fragrance and a scented candle, playing a round of golf or going for a pint with a friend?

This will help you to tap back into whatever makes you smile, relax and feel nurtured. As a parent, you are often so busy looking after, and nurturing, others that you neglect your own needs and start to run on empty. Looking after yourself is one of the key ingredients of being a great parent. Nurturing your needs and giving yourself 'time out' is a vital part of respecting yourself and valuing your very important role. It's really important to look after yourself first because then you will be in better shape – emotionally, physically and mentally – to look after your family positively.

Delegating

Let go of the idea of being the perfect parent. Being a perfectionist is unrealistic and exhausting and it also denies your child the broader experience of others contributing to their lives and doing things in different ways. One of the quickest ways to alleviate the feelings of being overwhelmed is to delegate jobs around the house. Young children love to help and can start by laying the table or putting their toys away. Teenagers can bring down their washing and can in fact turn on the washing machine if you show them how (as they are the most technically advanced children of a generation!) and partners really can load up the dishwasher, especially if they know it makes you smile more!

Be open and confident about asking, and also expecting, your family to be a team that's willing to pull together to help each other. Brainstorm all the jobs you currently do that could be shared out amongst your family and jot them down. Commit to making a couple of small changes to look after yourself, and watch your confidence, enthusiasm and happiness flourish and your family will too.

'We' Time

I am a great believer that working with your partner and working on your adult relationships builds up your confidence and takes away your sense of being overwhelmed. It's important to have a night out together regularly and to put it in your diary so that it really happens, as having children can hijack your relationships with your partner, friends or family, and feeling overwhelmed, undervalued and tired out can really damage your confidence over time.

No matter where you are in your relationship, it's important and healthy to regularly check in on it from time to time, to keep it fresh, growing and alive. Ask some simple but thought-provoking questions, such as:

- Where would you say you are with your partner at the moment, in terms of a happy, growing relationship?
- What do you think they would say in answer to that question – how would they describe your relationship at the moment?
- Imagine that you are taking a snapshot photo on your mobile phone of where your relationship is at the moment, What would you see in the bigger overview picture? Where is the relationship as a whole?

Ultimately it is up to you to find meaning in what you discover and learn, but decision-making is best done with good information. Here are some great questions to answer either on your own or as a couple, to take the temperature of your relationship from various angles and determine where it's heading. It's a good idea to consider using this questionnaire every six months or so. If you think this list is long, take a moment to consider its importance and the impact on your life if you don't answer these questions! So take your time and consider these great empowering questions:

What is your instant 'blink' about your relationship?

Malcolm Gladwell, in his great book *Blink*, talks about intuition and how we often make better decisions with snap judgements than we do with volumes of analysis or lots of justifications.

Many times, our snap judgements, first impressions, gut reactions and intuition offer a much better means of making sense of the world. So first ask yourself what your gut reaction is to the following aspects of your relationship:

1. Love

a. Is our love safe, healthy and happy?

b. Do I love who this person is now, as they are, flaws and all?

c. Am I in love with who they are, not just what they have, give, provide, do or who they know?

2. Self

a. Am I proud of who I am when I'm with this person?

b. Am I giving myself properly and my life fully to this commitment and person?

c. Am I willing to change, when it's important or necessary, to keep our relationship healthy and happy?

3. Future

a. Can I see myself with this person for the rest of my life?

b. Do I believe and/or know that we can build an amazing life together?

c. Do we share a similar vision of our future?

4. Character

a. Does this person have the character (values/morals/ethics) that I want in a wife/husband/partner?

b. Does this person have the character (accountability/responsibility/trustworthiness/honesty) that I want in a partner?

c. Do I love the way this person treats me and other people, even when no one is looking?

5. Friendship

a. Would I be friends with this person even if we weren't a couple?

b. Do I enjoy their company outside of intimacy and chemistry?

c. Can I see myself in friendship with this person when we're 90?

6. Communication

a. Does this person communicate in a healthy way regardless of highs and lows?

b. Is this person open and willing to talk about any and all of our challenges?

c. Do we enjoy talking, listening, joking, solving, brainstorming, planning and sharing?

7. Growth

a. Are we growing as individuals and together?

b. Do we share a similar vision on personal and relationship growth?

c. Do we make growth a priority in our lives?

8. Parenting

a. Am I happy in the direction we are both going with bringing up our children? Are we passing on similar values to our kids?

b. For new relationships and possible step-parents:
    Do I feel relaxed, confident and comfortable that this new person in my life is right for raising my children or disciplining them?

c.   Do my children love and trust this person and feel safe and comfortable with them?

9. Family

a.   Do we share similar views of how family is and will be in our lives?

b.   Are we creating the kind of family I am proud of?

c.   Do we make time for, appreciate and honour our families?

10. Health and fitness

a.   Do we share similar views on health and fitness?

b.   Are we healthy together?

c.   Do we lift each other higher in health, fitness and wellness?

11. Finances

a.   Is this person responsible and trustworthy with money?

b.   Do we have similar financial expectations?

c.   Am I comfortable with the income they make today and could make tomorrow?

12. Quality of life

a.   Do we have similar views about quality of life?

b.   Do we believe in and create a healthy balance in our lives?

c.   Are we committed to what matters most (love, family, friends, faith, spirituality, etc.)?

13. Contribution

a.   Do we give or volunteer?

b.   Are we doing our part to help create a better world?

c.   Are we teaching our kids the importance of contribution?

14. Fun

a. When I think of our relationship, can I say we have fun together?

b. Do we enjoy similar activities, hobbies, sports, adventures?

c. Do we have fun even when we're not doing anything specific?

15. Friends

a. Do we enjoy each other's friends?

b. Do we have healthy and uplifting friendships?

c. Are we willing to end a friendship to protect our relationship?

16. Change

a. Are we both aware of and open to changes in life?

b. Are we talking about and preparing for change?

c. Do we see change as healthy and normal for our relationship?

17. Spiritual/religious

a. Are we similar in our beliefs?

b. Do we appreciate, honour and support our similarities and differences?

c. Do we communicate our beliefs and values well to our children?

18. Lifestyle

a. Do we hold similar views about lifestyle?

b. Do we have a healthy, happy and sustainable lifestyle?

c. Are we willing to do what it takes together, to get the lifestyle we want/deserve?

19. Finally ask:

a. What did you discover from the questionnaire?

b. How does that make you feel?

c. Does anything need to happen now?

If you feel something needs to change, take a few minutes to consider the best way to share this opinion with your partner and give them the space to go through this questionnaire before you blast them with your thoughts. When would be a good time to have a healthy and respectful discussion about what you discovered? Is it when the kids are in bed, you've got a babysitter and gone out for a quiet meal to chat or when you've had a bit more time to think about what to do next?

Doing this exercise will help you to keep connected, and sharing, talking and laughing together as you raise your children, which is often a side of parenting that's overlooked and is vital to your sense of wellbeing and confidence.

Celebrating Your Successes

Another important thing to do as a parent is to stop and pat yourself on the back from time to time, as it builds up your confidence and sense of achievement. Most of us never stop to think how we are doing, but it's really important to do this regularly, as it makes you realise how well you are doing, instead of beating yourself up all the time and feeling guilty.

I encourage the parents I work with to buy a special journal or notebook and to call it 'My Success Diary' and to keep it by their bedside so that they can write in it regularly. For now, write down every success that you've EVER had, from passing your driving test, passing an exam, learning to skate or salsa dance, or designing your own garden, to changing a nappy for the first time or watching your teenager being patient with their grandmother. Acknowledge every single success you've ever had in your life and remember the everyday successes as well as the big moments about being a parent. Keep on writing and writing and writing, and then take a bow. You deserve this moment!

This is your Success Diary and you need to acknowledge your large and small successes, as they keep you positive, upbeat and motivated and it's VERY IMPORTANT to congratulate yourself regularly as it keeps you moving forward in your adventure as a parent.

Your Success Diary will probably become your most treasured possession as it provides you with every support you need to achieve one big or small goal after another. Keep your Success Diary near you, and when you feel your confidence wobbling, take it out and have a look at all your successes. Keep on adding to this Success Diary over the months and years ahead.

The Importance of Getting the Balance Right

In all my years of working with successful parents, I've found that their biggest motivators are their personal life and their family. Two people in particular stand out to me, as both were incredibly successful, wealthy and influential but one was happy and energetic and the other was angry and depressed. Can you guess what set them apart?

The happy woman had made time to spend with her partner and children regularly and consistently. She felt good about her success because she was able to share it with the people who were the most important to her. The other was a workaholic and was never able to make time for her family and friends. Even though she wanted to connect with them, she always had too much to do.

So the key question to ask yourself each evening is: 'Have I spent enough time with my family lately?' as it will focus you on the important things in your life. We all lead busy lives, but it's crucial to make time to spend with the ones you love, while still accomplishing your most important tasks.

8

Helping Your Children Gain Independence

From the moment your children are playing 'peek-a-boo', you're preparing them for independence, and getting them ready to take responsibility for their actions and to face consequences. As parents, you are always in the process of letting go of your children and it is often difficult to accept. You need to allow them to make their own mistakes and help them understand the pressures of the real world.

You can't expect your children to suddenly 'become independent' if you don't begin this process gradually, and from an early age. Children need to know that independence means facing failure and disappointment, and involves taking risks. You owe it to them to let these be gentle experiences and lessons in life. It is a balance, like everything else, between being overprotective and too liberal.

Solving Problems and Allowing Choices

Independence can start as early on as you choose, from letting your child try to do up his coat buttons to deciding for themselves what colour jumper they want to wear, to allowing your teenager to drive himself to the party.

If you overdo the amount you do for your children, you give them a massive feeling of helplessness, worthlessness, frustration, resentment and even anger. Of course this needs to be balanced by their age and stage of development. Just think how it must feel to be six years old and hear your parents saying to you, 'Eat up all your peas,' 'Let me do up your zip,' 'You're tired out, go and have a sleep,' 'I think you should go to the loo now...' Or imagine you are fourteen years old and over the course of a day you hear your parents tell you: 'Hold your knife and fork properly – like this,' 'Don't spill baked beans down your T-shirt,' 'Don't wear that jacket; it doesn't match your shirt.'

What would your reaction be if your partner kept telling you and reminding you to do things all day long? Probably not printable!

Patronising isn't it, and humiliating and unnecessary? So it's probably true that you wouldn't want your kids to harbour those feelings towards you. Remember, it's a balance between genuinely helping your kids when things are a bit overwhelming and diffi-cult and allowing them to experiment, make mistakes and learn from them in a safe environment. You owe it to them to help them become responsible, independent adults able to cope on their own.

If a child's struggle is respected they learn tenacity and self-respect. So it's often by just waiting and encouraging your child that you can help them develop this attitude to life. You need to introduce your kids to problem-solving and the ability to weigh up the pros and cons and look at a situation from both sides. It helps them to tackle issues for themselves later on. Your children need to be well prepared for real life: robust, confident and resilient. So being a flexible parent means recognising where the balance lies in allowing your child to replace your rules with their judgement.

There is no 'exact' answer for when this starts to evolve, because every child is different and matures at their own speed. They handle responsibility in their own way and in their own time. The best answer is to spend lots of time getting to know your own kids then you'll know naturally how to handle this new shift in responsibility.

Here are some questions to ponder:

- What needs to change for you to move easily into this different role of delegating some responsibilities to your kids?
- What stumbling blocks may get in your way? What do you need to do to get round them?
- In what ways do you need to change, develop or grow to make way for your child's emerging autonomy? Would developing a hobby, getting a new job or learning a new skill help you through this transition?

Don't jump in to rescue

Growing up and becoming independent and autonomous is all about letting your child make their own mistakes appropriate to their age and development. The ultimate goal is that they one day function on their own, away from you, as an independent adult.

Don't always jump in to rescue them. Let your kids wobble and fall off the climbing frame in the garden (if it's not too dangerous!), make a cake that falls apart and try to figure out how to assemble their flat-pack shelving for their room...if they're old enough!

One way to develop their thinking skills is not to rush in with all the answers. When children ask questions (which can be rather a lot at around three years old) give them a chance to think things through for themselves and to formulate their own ideas and concepts of the world. So when your four-year-old says, 'Why does Nanny always come to visit us every week on a Wednesday?', ask the question back as a rhetorical question to see what your child comes up with: 'So why *does* Nanny always come over on a Wednesday – what do you think?'

Letting things go is quite a hard skill to develop at first as you will naturally want to rush in to answer their question, but by standing back you are helping your child think for themselves, and offering them an opportunity to grow, learn and feel a sense of personal achievement.

Don't dash their dreams

It's natural and honourable for parents to want to protect their children from disappointments and failures, but this can ultimately have a negative effect and may mean they aren't taught to strive for or dream of doing something that currently seems out of reach. It can prevent kids from being confident enough to go beyond their comfort zone, which can stifle their aims and aspirations later on in life. You may now be wondering what's so bad about helping them or solving their problems. But the trouble with this approach is that if your child depends on you for everything in life, they lose all confidence and belief in their own judgement, and can often find over time that they suffer from feelings of inadequacy and anger.

So when your child comes home and says, 'I want to earn some money working in the local newsagent,' think about the way you respond to their aspirations for independence in the way you speak to them. Don't dash their dreams with: 'Well, that's hardly likely because you'll never be punctual enough for that. Look at last weekend – you didn't wake up till midday!' Try saying, 'So you think you might like a part-time job. Tell me about it.'

If they suddenly say, 'I want to be a lawyer when I grow up,' don't dash their dreams with: 'Gosh, with the comments I read on your last school report? Dream on.' Try saying, 'So you're considering a career as a lawyer. Tell me about that idea.'

Although these responses may sound obvious, there really is a skill involved here as it takes determination and a conscious step back to talk to children like this and to encourage their independence by the way you speak to them. Try communicating in these ways and see how your relationships easily and effortlessly transform.

Think What Your Child is Thinking

Embrace the wider implications of your child's actions. You need to get 'inside' the mind of someone your child's age and try to have empathy. If you can understand your son's newfound obsession with shutting his bedroom door, because he's discovered privacy, then you'll understand why he loses the plot when you walk into his room without knocking. Remember what it felt like being told off by a teacher, or falling out with your best friend at school? Then you'll naturally say the right thing to your daughter when she comes home one night in a flood of tears.

Parenting is not about winning and losing, it's about helping your child develop self-confidence in a healthy, balanced way. Sometimes it is about you changing, stepping back, being mature and magnanimous and staying flexible. Bear in mind that adjusting your parenting style to match your children's temperament is also useful when you're developing your child's confidence. Because flexibility is so important in parenting to create self-belief, it is worth remembering that if you don't change with your child, they are just going to move on without you; and let's face it, that would be a terrible thing to happen. Don't try to hold on to your youth by treating your child as if they aren't really growing up. I know it's cheaper than having a facelift, but it doesn't serve your child in the long run!

Are your children all the same?

It always makes me smile to see how a parent's attitude changes once they've had a second child. First-time parents are invariably staunch believers in the nurturing side of the debate. They are confident that the experiences they've created for their child have made them what, or who, they are. The second child then comes along, and the parents may look at the two children's personalities and realise that they are like chalk and cheese – even though they've been raised in the same way. One may be placid, the other highly strung. One tidy, the other totally untidy. One may take easily to new situations, the other doesn't like change. One may need hardly any sleep, the other needs 12 hours.

It becomes obvious that nature is contributing to your child's development, as well as nurture. As a parent you must take this properly into account and accept it to build self-confidence. A wary child can't help being wary, and an active child can't help being active. The skill is to create situations that take advantage of your child's natural strengths and avoid accentuating their weaknesses.

Remember this when, for example, you want your children to help around the house. Give your kids as many choices about what to do as possible and use this as an opportunity to discover their preferences. Let them choose amongst themselves the jobs you have for them, or if you want to encourage them to participate in school activities, encourage them to choose between a variety of things to do and support their choices even if they aren't what you would pick. Otherwise, you belittle their self-esteem and make them feel a failure. Again, don't fight your child's temperament – celebrate and work with it to create a happy, relaxed, self-confident child, comfortable with his own temperament.

One Step Forwards, Two Steps Back

Children don't develop in straight lines. As it is a gradual process, it is worth remembering that a lot of development occurs in spurts. Sometimes your child is developing psychologically in sprints – they rest and recover, then they sprint ahead again, racing, resting and recovering again. The challenge for you, as the parent, is to recognise that your child is going through a major development transition and is not jogging along at a steady pace. It is really hard to know what to expect from one day to the next.

Most parents accept such change when their children are younger, but they forget that it is like this throughout childhood and adolescence, too. One afternoon, going to a football match, my daughter completely lost it because we didn't seem to offer her something to drink in the car and she claimed that we always ignore her and leave her out. Yet later on that same afternoon, on the way home, she said how much she loved us and how lucky she was to have such lovely parents. She wasn't being deliberately fickle (I remembered to mutter under my breath!) but was going through a transitional phase. The challenge was not to point out the inconsistency to her because nothing would be gained by it. We just accepted her love graciously but recognised the mixture of mature and immature thinking.

It's like a business that has been taken over by a new company, which is implementing new structures. Sometimes the old habits die hard, and these habits still surface while everyone adapts to the new system. It's the same with children. Things get out of sync. Show patience and understanding – it will pass.

The Three Stages of Maturity

The areas that seem most difficult for a parent to accept are the transitions in maturity. They can seem like losses, rather than just changes. There are three broad stages of development: early childhood, middle childhood and adolescence (see Ages and Stages in Chapter 6) and each age and stage requires you to adapt your parenting to handle your growing child's physical, mental, social and emotional development.

As your children grow and mature there will be times when you need to give your parenting style an MOT to see if you are aware of your child's changing needs, as these changes will make a difference in your parenting. Just as your child is maturing and developing, your attitudes and feelings will also change, so it's important to be aware from time to time of what you are doing so that you can make sure your parenting style is still working for all of you. Each one of your children will develop at their own pace and this will make a difference in your parenting as well. Make sure that the boundaries and expectations you set are good for their challenges and match their maturity. I believe that with a little reflection you can easily find what's best for them at each age and stage. Growing up is not a competition, so just relax and accept where your child is.

There will be many times throughout your child's life when you will have to make parenting choices so keep in mind that you are trying to make your child as independent, resilient, relaxed and confident as you can, and that your parenting style will probably be a mixture of more than one approach. Trust your intuition and you'll handle the transitions with ease.

The first shift is from you being the absolute centre of their life, to being one of many people they care about. The fact that your daughter wants to spend more time with her friends and less with you doesn't mean she doesn't love you. It just means she is developing her social circle and widening her relationships. You are going to have to share her. If you see this transition as sad, and a loss, then that's what it will feel like. If you see it as a pleasure that she is growing up and able to establish independent friendships, then it will be a source of pride to you. It's all about your perception.

The second transition is when your role as a parent moves from one of complete control to helping your child control their own life. This can be a hard lesson for a parent to learn. Your role has to change from dominance to option-based. For example, when I now take my 16-year-old daughter shopping, she chooses her own clothes (within reason), whereas when she was five I used to choose all of her clothes. I may not like the colour of her T-shirt, but it's more important for me to see her develop her own confidence and a style for herself and to learn to make her own decisions. Changing to a more flexible approach can be difficult if you feel a loss of authority, and it may make you feel powerless. Step back and practise with small things like letting them choose lunch from the menu, the colour of their trousers or their duvet cover.

The third transition is a tough one, too, for some parents – letting your child develop into their own individual person. That means with their own opinions, style of dressing, taste in music, differences in politics, and ultimately their own career and lifestyle.

I think it is helpful to understand that each stage of development could have a central question attached to it.

- Infancy: 'How can I help my child feel more secure?'
- Toddlerhood: 'How can I help my child feel more in control?'
- Early childhood: 'What can I do to help my child feel more grown-up?'
- Junior school: 'How can I help my child feel more competent and capable?'
- Early teen: 'How can I help my teenager feel more independent?'
- Late teen: 'How can I help my adolescent understand him- or herself better?'

Many people describe raising a child like a bird learning to fly or a boat being built, ready to be launched. Whatever your analogy is, it is what your job as a parent is really all about – creating a healthy, happy, self-confident, independent adult. The issue here is not *whether* your role as a parent will change; it has to, because your child's development demands it. Accepting change and your changing role is one of the hardest things you will ever have to do as a parent, but it is actually one of the most important aspects of building self-confidence for your child.

'Conveying our love to our children is priority number one. It needs to come before any other aspect of the parenting process. Kids don't care how much you know, until they know how much you care. Before you offer correction, guidance, or suggestions, your unconditional love needs to be the basis of your relationship with your children.'
~ Stephanie Marston

How You Act Really Matters

A useful attitude to adopt is one about which I spoke about in Chapter 6, but it is also relevant here: 'awareness parenting'. This means being constantly aware of the bigger picture. It's the destination of your parenting – the creation of a unique, confident adult – that really matters. So many parents are simply reactive and casual. By being aware, you react with intention, rather than by chance. It doesn't mean you are predictable and can't be spontaneous or natural, but you hold the vision of where you are trying to get to together.

There are usually three situations where you have to be aware of how you are reacting and how you are making decisions:

1. When you have plenty of time to think

The first situation is when you have plenty of time to think through what you want to do, before you act. Such as when choosing a secondary school or deciding whether your son should take lessons in judo now that he is showing a keen interest in it. You have plenty of time to reflect on the effect that your decision will have on your child. It is an informed decision, not an impulsive one. This means that the decisions you reach are considered and thought through and you feel very confident in them.

2. When you have to react more quickly

The second situation is when you have to react on the spot, with little time. Your two-year-old toddler refuses to eat what you've served her for dinner; your eleven-year-old wants to have a sleepover tonight and rings you at work. Here, you have to remember your principles and respond in a consistent way, and because you have made being aware into your habit, you can do it quickly and in keeping with your parenting style.

3. When you have no time to think

The third situation is when you have a completely reflex reaction. Your toddler has thrown a wobbly by the sweets in Tesco; your 10-year-old has just tried to strangle her 12-year-old brother; or your teenage daughter has gone upstairs to her bedroom with her new boyfriend to listen to some music.

An aware parent will relax, breathe deeply, use my One Point Technique (see page 62) and see the bigger picture. They will stay grounded with their toddler, speak specifically about what the 10-year-old has to do next to calm the situation with her 12-year-old brother or tell their teenage daughter to go into the sitting room with her boyfriend.

If you have developed the habit of being an aware parent, handling these situations will become second nature. I always think that keeping a sense of humour is enormously valuable. It defuses tension, lifts your mood and widens everyone's perspective. We all take a great deal of time over buying a new house, car or washing machine, yet many adults never really take time to consider what they're doing when they are raising their children.

It doesn't come naturally to many people, and thinking about what you're doing doesn't take away all the fun and spontaneity. If you are a thoughtful parent, you are nurturing self-esteem, all the time. The way you nurture your children influences how their genetic nature is allowed to be expressed. It's not just in their DNA.

Remember, you are a role model

You have the ability to influence your child's personality, interests, character, intelligence, attitudes and values. You can even influence their likes and dislikes. You can influence how your child behaves at school, at home and with friends; whether he is kind, considerate, judgemental or selfish. What you do definitely matters!

When you are an anxious parent, you convey that anxiety to your child, because you transmit that energy. When you are a confident, relaxed, chilled parent, your child watches that and learns from you. Children actually have a strong desire to grow up to be just like their mum and dad! If you are courteous, kind, friendly, generous and spirited, your child will turn out similarly. If you are rude, judgemental, aggressive and aloof, your child will learn to be the same – this is particularly true before adolescence. So be careful when you scream profanities at your husband when he can't find his keys to the car again. You are a role model, whether you like it or not.

Don't be afraid to assert authority as a parent – that's what you're there for. Rather than telling yourself you are powerless against the influence of the media or your children's friends, remember that you do have a strong, guiding influence over your child. So manage it and remember it is because of these outside influences that your role is even more important. Limit your child's TV and video games and regulate what they are allowed to watch. Remember to have clear, fair, consistent boundaries.

Understand Your Child's Needs

In order to be good parents we must have realistic expectations and delicately balance our own needs, as well as our children's. It takes patience and understanding, and we all have basic needs that must be met before we can realise our dreams. Until your children can meet their own needs you must do it for them. You have to help them learn how to take care of themselves.

There are five levels of basic needs, and each level supports the next – like the layers in a pyramid. If one need is not being met, it is very difficult to move up to the next one. In summary, the five levels of needs are:

1. Survival: basic needs such as food and water
2. Security: the need for safety and shelter
3. Social: the need to belong
4. Esteem: the need to feel one's self-worth developing
5. Self-actualisation: the need for personal growth beyond physical development

These basic concepts are based on Dr Abraham Maslow's 'hierarchy of needs' theory. These needs continue throughout your child's life, and it can take a lifetime of effort for children and parents to reach the top of the pyramid. Some never do. It takes great patience, good communication, lots of love and maybe a sprinkling of luck. There are never any guarantees in life, and even good parents make mistakes and need to be prepared for disappointments.

The more you are aware of these important needs of your child and understand the responsibilities of parenting, the more it is likely that your child will reach their full potential and live the highest vision of what is possible.

Level 2 of Maslow's hierarchy of needs is for children to feel safe and secure. Creating a safe haven or a real home is very important to children, as it is a place to relax, be messy, play, chat to family, create, discover, unwind, have privacy, be alone and be themselves completely. It is predictable in its familiarity. It is not only a place of love, security and protection, but also a place to respect.

We all have a need to feel protection from physical harm and freedom from fear. Children thrive on routine, security and rules. If your child feels insecure, he'll be reluctant to try out new challenges. Children are very sensitive, and they need your unconditional love and protection.

The thing to remember is that children of all ages need structure and limits. The actual day-to-day rules vary according to their age and level of maturity. It's fine to establish different rules for different children in your family, as long as you explain why the rules vary. If they are based on real differences between the children and genuinely warrant different treatments, then everyone will understand and you won't be accused of being unfair.

Let's look at what I mean by this. One reason for a different rule could be that one child is older than another, so it helps to explain to the younger child that she can look forward to the same rule when she is the same age as her brother. Perhaps one child has trouble completing homework and needs more supervision than his brother. The homework rules must be the same, i.e. get the homework done on time and regularly, but one child can do it in his room or on the computer independently, while the other one needs you to sit with him. Most children actually understand this reasoning, and get upset only if their treatment is unjustified or unfair.

There are plenty of reasons to have rules, but the main reason is that over time they help your children develop the ability to manage their own behaviour. Strange as this may seem, your child's ability to control himself grows out of his ability to be controlled by you. Over time, your child's behaviour gradually shifts from being external (imposed by you) to being internal (imposed by himself). The rules your child learns from you shape the rules he applies to himself.

You Choose Your Response!

It's only natural for a child to test your rules to the limit. She is striving for some control over her own life, but your job as a parent is to do what is right for your child. You know what is best for her and you have her best interests at heart. You're also more experienced and wiser. You can see the bigger picture and her judgement isn't as good as yours. Just remember, you are there to help her gain understanding. So remember sometimes to press your pause button. When your child challenges you, it's easy to get caught up in the moment and say things you don't mean, things you later regret. We all do it, but it is helpful to remember that you have a pause button – something that enables you to stop between what happened, or was said, and your response to it.

With practice, you can develop this as a habit and a way of helping you cope under pressure. Stop, pause, take a deep breath, relax and be firm. Stand your ground, if you know you're right. Just think about the word responsible – response(able) – able to choose your own response. Remember to use your imaginary pause button as it can really make a difference.

If you are not firm and give in too easily because it's just easier, think about the long-term repercussions of your actions. How can you instil tenacity in your child on their journey in life if you give in so easily? If you give in because your child whines, nags, sulks or argues back, then this is just going to make them whine, nag, sulk and argue more because they know that if they keep it up long enough you'll give in! Any child can figure that out. Secondly, you send a message that your rules don't matter.

If you don't like your child being angry with you, is it because you just want to be your child's friend and not their parent? It's okay for your child to be angry with you for a good decision you've made. It really is! A child who wants to stay up to watch the Champions League Semi-Final until 10:30pm is not going to be in good humour, or any use, at school the next day. If you have a loving, balanced relationship generally, a little dispute really won't damage that.

It's important that your child sees that your authority comes from your wisdom and good judgement. It's a good idea sometimes to re-examine your rules to see if they still have logic and fairness and are relevant to the current age of your child. Sometimes children simply grow out of a rule. But remember, the decision to change or adapt a rule is your decision, not your child's. Being firm but fair is all there is to it.

Spending Quality Time with Your Child

- What's your child's favourite subject and activity at school?
- Who are your child's best friends?
- What are the names of your child's teachers?
- How's your child feeling at the moment? Relaxed, happy, sad, popular, lonely, anxious, troubled, stressed?
- Can you name your child's heroes, in sport, music, films, books or on TV?
- Do you know what book your child is reading (or even if they are reading!)?

If you don't know the answers to these questions, it may be a sign that you could become a bit more involved in your child's life. It could help them do better at school, feel better about themselves, have greater self-esteem as they feel cherished and nurtured. It doesn't matter how old your child is – they need your involvement, and that means spending time with them.

A good reason why it's so important to spend time with your children is that you can never predict when they're going to want to share things with you, or open up and talk. My son would never open up in the car on the way home from school, especially when he was tired and hungry, even if I directly asked him how his day was. It was always at other times, when we were just around the house or doing something else together. So spending more time with your child means you're more likely to be there when they suddenly decide they want to reveal the details about what happened at school today, a joke someone told them or the lovely feedback they got for their English homework.

By going to football matches, rounders matches, swimming galas, netball tournaments or piano recitals, you're showing your commitment, interest and reassurance to your child – and by driving a crowd of their friends to bowling, you hear all the conversations naturally.

Parenting is not something you can pick and choose when to do. It takes hard work and often means you have to rearrange meetings, if you're a working parent; but when your child has left home you won't say, 'I wish I had spent more time at work!' You'll wish you'd spent more time with your child when they were still around.

To me, quality time doesn't mean watching over my children's homework or hot housing them. I'm their parent, not their school teacher. Yes, I take an interest in their school work and will help if they need it, but then we like to cook, take the dogs for a walk, listen to music and go shopping for clothes and shoes. Quality time isn't dictated by the things you are doing, it's down to the ways in which you do them. It is not a list of learning outcomes; it's about how you approach something – it's about being prepared to fully engage and really listen to your children, to enjoy sharing a passion or a hobby with them, playing easily and naturally with them, and just being relaxed and having fun with them.

It doesn't work if you'd rather be somewhere else. If that's where you are mentally, then you're better off actually going there! That's not quality time spent with your child. Your child knows when you're genuinely interested or if you're on autopilot, so be there both mentally and physically. They'll get more from an hour with you fully engaged than they will from several hours of you pretending. Try to become interested in what interests your child – not what you are interested in, or think your child should be interested in. Swap your thinking around. Be led by your children's interests and hobbies. It helps their self-esteem and maturity, and you will learn lots of new things.

Encouraging Autonomy

From the first day at school, first sleepover and first school trip to France, to the day they leave home, you are preparing your child for separation from you. It is a step-by-step, gradual movement out into the big world, where they can be confident and independent from you.

Good parenting requires a balance between involvement and independence, and your child learns self-confidence from learning to be self-sufficient. Ask yourself these three questions to help develop your child's independence:

1. Does my child have the capabilities to handle this situation, or make this decision, on their own?

2. If my child handles this on her own successfully, will she come away feeling better about herself, or will she have learnt something really important as a result?

3. If my child makes a mistake, will the consequences be something we can all live with in the long run?

Parents who encourage independence in their children help them to develop a sense of self-direction. To be successful in life, children need both self-control and self-direction. They also need self-discipline to balance their own individual needs with the needs of others. It is perfectly normal for children to push for autonomy and push the boundaries. It's not always about rebelliousness and disobedience. It is about your child's need to feel in control of his own life and not feel constantly controlled by someone else. Children need to feel a mixture of freedom and constraints.

Here are some of my top tips and suggestions of things you can try:

- Pick the right battles and remember to be flexible as your child moves from one stage of development to the next.
- Give your child a limited choice between two things. This builds your child's confidence, but really, you have already pre-approved your child's choices.
- Praise your child's decision, as this is very important in building confidence in their own decision-making choices.
- Help your child think their decisions through and don't always give them the answer.
- Let your child make their own mistakes. We often step in too soon to avoid disappointment, but a child can gain much from the experience if we let them. By ensuring your child feels supported but not smothered, you're helping to develop their self-confidence.

There's a big difference between being an involved parent and being a parent who does too much. Take the issue of homework, for example, an issue close to my heart as a former teacher. When your child is young, help them to learn the discipline of homework and make sure they allocate enough time for it, understand what is being asked, and that it is done well. In the early years of homework, it is about developing good habits – a regular time, a clean table, the right equipment and support if they need help. But as your child gets older, they must learn to manage these tasks for themselves. They must learn what is expected of them and what is mediocre or top-notch work. Then the focus is on the habit of homework and where they do it. It is about allowing your children to accept responsibility for their own work. In secondary school, your involvement should be limited to when you are explicitly asked to help, if you can. Again, the key is about being flexible and changing as your child develops and matures.

It is only natural for your child to seek independence from you, and you need to stay flexible in granting them autonomy. If you can exercise it in a way that allows you to maintain ultimate control, then you have both won. The arguments that may arise while your child is striving toward independence are a pain, but actually, if you stand back and look at the destination of your parenting, it is a desirable trait in your child. Too much passivity isn't a good thing to encourage in a child, as it robs them of control, and ultimately their self-esteem and confidence in handling the world. When they challenge your way of doing things, your child is showing you that they are an individual and that they are growing up.

To develop self-esteem, children need psychological space. If you are too emotionally wrapped up in your child's life, they will feel smothered and overprotected. They will not flourish. It's all about achieving a balance. Children need to feel attached emotionally to their parents but also separate from them. Children have a right to their own emotions and feelings. They need to sort out for themselves how they feel about things. Remember, children need some emotional privacy, and they don't always feel like talking. Just be ready and available when they do.

It may seem a horrible thought when your child is just learning to walk or talk, and it probably seems many years away, but your ultimate aim as parents is to set your children free – to let them fly the nest, if you like, and make their own way in the world as well-balanced adults, ready to take on the role of being parents themselves. For you, as parents, there is no greater reward than to see your child become an adult of whom you are really proud!

Concluding Thoughts

By now, you will have got a flavour of what my parent coaching is all about. It's about focusing on the future, setting yourself some parenting goals and breaking the goals down into bite-sized, baby steps that feel manageable.

It means finding new and different ways to do things, that are grounded and positive, and increasing your flexibility and your choices. It's about recognising that you're doing your best, exploring your skills or learning some new ones and letting go of the idea of being perfect.

But most of all, successful parenting is learning to stay confident and in control.

Every family is individual and it is important to find your own parenting style to suit you and your family; you shouldn't feel that you need to measure up to other families who seem to be getting it 'right'.

My intention throughout this book has been to empower you with new ideas, fresh thinking, and simple and practical strategies, tips and techniques to help **you** bring out **your** answers for **your** family and gain clarity, direction and confidence in your parenting, in a non-judgemental and non-critical way, so that you feel empowered with your own answers and ways of doing things that work for your family.

Bringing up children is not an exact science and, as my mum used to say, everyone is an expert in bringing up other people's children, so just relax, stay positive and learn to be the best parent you can be for your children so that their memories of childhood are happy ones.

One Last Thing

May I ask you a favour?

If you have got anything out of this book, if you highlighted or circled or Post-it-noted, or had an 'Aha' moment, I'm hoping you'll do something for me.

Give this copy to someone else.

Ask them to read it. Beg them to make a choice about being the best parent they can be for their kids.

The world needs good parents, so that we can all bring up happy, confident kids, who go on to be happy, confident teenagers, who go on to be happy, confident adults, who go on to be happy, confident parents – like a positive ripple in a pond…

Spread the word.

Thank you.

www.TheSueAtkins.com

Index

About the Author

Sue Atkins is a parenting expert and coach, who is dedicated to spreading her message about good parenting. A former deputy head teacher, with over 22 years' experience working with both parents and children, Sue is also a qualified NLP Master Practitioner and Trainer and has been taught by Dr Richard Bandler – the co-founder and creator of NLP in association with Paul McKenna Training. In addition to running one-to-one parent coaching sessions, Sue is a regular speaker at events and workshops and regularly appears on the TV and radio.